THE · SEAL · OF · THE · DIOCESE · OF · VIRGINIA · 1607 · 1785 ·

CONFITEMINI DOMINO

NEAR THE FALLS

Two Hundred Years
of
The Falls Church

BY

THE REVEREND JOSEPH HODGE ALVES,
RECTOR OF THE FALLS CHURCH

AND

MR. HAROLD SPELMAN, SENIOR WARDEN
EMERITUS AND HISTORIOGRAPHER OF
THE FALLS CHURCH

THE FALLS CHURCH
FALLS CHURCH, VIRGINIA
1969

Edited by Helen Eldridge Vogel
Special Drawings by Elizabeth Pyle Jones Beatty
Photographic Work by Lee Briggs
Photo Processing by Porter Studios

Designed and printed in the U.S.A., by
The Turnpike Press, Inc.
Annandale, Virginia

taBle of contents

A 12-page section containing 24 illustrations follows page 38

Drawings illustrating church activities in the 1890's will be found on pages 52 and 56.

* * *

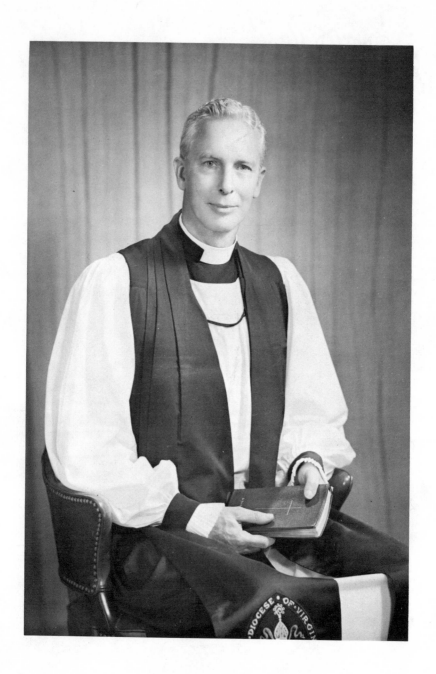

fOREWORO

The Diocese of Virginia is thankful to Almighty God for the two hundred years of faithful and fruitful service rendered by The Falls Church. We in Virginia are justly proud of our long history, and of beautiful and venerable Colonial buildings, of which the Falls Church is an outstanding example. But even more proud are we that The Falls Church has always continued to be a vigorous and vital parish church, teeming with Christian worship and missionary zeal, changing and growing with the times. May this be always true.

It is my privilege to congratulate the Clergy, Vestry and People in this Bicentennial Celebration. May God's richest blessings continue upon The Falls Church in the years to come.

Bishop of Virginia

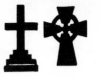

THE FALLS CHURCH · 1769

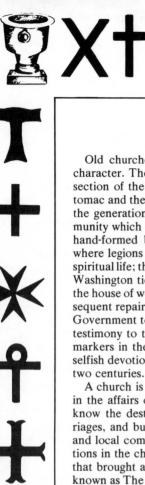

pReface

Old churches like old towns develop their own individual character. The "Church on the road to the falls" at the intersection of the old road to the ferry below the falls of the Potomac and the road to Alexandria has left its special imprint on the generations that have worshipped there and on the community which bears its name. Such vestiges are apparent in the hand-formed bricks from the local kiln; the baptismal font, where legions of infants, children and adults have begun their spiritual life; the giant white oak, where legend has it that George Washington tied his horse when he attended Vestry meetings; the house of worship desecrated by an occupying army, and subsequent repairs to the structure made by a sympathetic Federal Government to help assuage the bitterness of defeat; the mute testimony to those who have gone on to eternal rest of grave markers in the churchyard; and the frequently unnoticed, unselfish devotion of men and women over a period of more than two centuries.

A church is more than a building. . .It remains a living hand in the affairs of men. . .It is a house of beginnings. Who can know the destinies set in motion with the Christenings, marriages, and burials that took place there? How many reforms and local community innovations were the result of conversations in the churchyard after services? The same zealous spirit that brought about the erection of the now venerable building known as The Falls Church has remained alive and has passed from father to son, from old-timer to newcomer and stranger, and from rector to parish. All of these interwoven skeins have gone into the warp and woof which make up the tapestry of the history of The Falls Church.

James Scott Rawlings in his *Virginia's Colonial Churches: An Architectural Guide,* says in his chapter concerning this historic structure, "Some of our colonial churches may seem to be overpraised and overcited in relation to their sister colonial churches. It is the other way round with The Falls Church."

To assist in making up for this deficiency, this history, *Near the Falls,* has been diligently researched and written by Harold J. Spelman, Senior Warden Emeritus and Historiographer, the author of the section from colonial times to the end of the War Between the States, and the Rector, The Rev. J. Hodge Alves, who has carried the narrative from that war up to the present day. We recognize that "What's past is prologue. . ."

acknowledgements

The principal sources for this history of The Falls Church for the period prior to 1800 are the minutes of Truro and Fairfax Parishes. From 1800 to 1873 we are indebted almost entirely to the *Virginia Village*, published in 1904, and the typewritten manuscript, *The Falls Church, 1733-1940*, both by the late Charles A. Stewart (1861-1950), Honorary Senior Warden.

The written records of The Falls Church prior to 1873 have been lost. From 1874 the Vestry minutes and parish registers are available and are supplemented by Mr. Stewart's manuscript on Falls Church through 1938. From 1948 the bound volumes of the church bulletins provide a record. In addition, the *Recollections* by Maude Morse and William Fitzhugh Edmonds, and the *Reminiscences* of the late G.D. Gordon Nicolson (1878-1961), long-time vestryman and Registrar supplement available material. Sources of background information are listed below.

The Rev. W.L. Ribble and the Rev. Francis W. Hayes, both former rectors, have contributed much to the periods of their services. The Rev. Melvin Steadman, Jr., has given generously of his knowledge and advice.

We are especially thankful to Mrs. Harvey Vogel for her work of editing and putting together the various parts, preparing the manuscript for publication, and generally carrying out the job. We record our thanks to the members of the Library Guild of The Falls Church for their work in indexing the manuscript.

We are grateful to Mrs. David Beatty and to Miss Kasha Larew for their sketches and drawings, and we wish to thank Mr. Lee Briggs for preparing some of the pictures included.

Our grateful thanks go to Mrs. Harold Manning, Mrs. Alan Humphreys, Mrs. Roy Franklin and Mrs. H.W. Jones for preparing the typewritten manuscripts, and to Mrs. Josephine Alves for checking many parts of them.

Finally, our thanks go to the members of the Vestry, the Bicentennial Committee and the Women of The Falls Church for their encouragement and help.

We dedicate this book to the memory of Charles A. Stewart and G.D. Gordon Nicolson.

Falls Church, Virginia   Harold J. Spelman
February, 1969   Senior Warden Emeritus

the falls chuRch fRom
its colonial Beginnings
1734
to the end of
the waR Between the states
1865

Virginians take special pride in their contributions to the history
of their country. They look backward at their heritage with satisfaction, but they are not unmindful of their role in the Twentieth
Century and their responsibility to those who will come later. So it
is that as the Congregation of The Falls Church in 1969 observes the
two hundredth anniversary of the completion of the historic old
structure in 1769, it rededicates itself to striving "to enkindle, map
and develop new missionary and evangelistic programs. These programs will be strengthened by emphasizing the Christian community,
nation and world." With these goals in mind for the future let us turn
back the pages of history to the very foundations of the history of
The Falls Church.

Rev. Melvin Steadman in his book *Falls Church By Fence and
Fireside* points out that "Fairfax County was settled by a cross section of wayward and aimless persons, as well as the straight-laced
and narrow. . . An endless procession both motley and dignified,
yeoman and cavalier, indentured and free, made its way painfully
over trails. . .The countryside was marked by contrast, a virgin land
which was the scene of great achievements, personal triumphs and
significant contributions to human progress. . .The early settlers set
a pattern for gracious living. . .Statesmen imbued with the spirit of
this new world formulated principles of individual liberty and etched
them deep on the surface of American life."[1] Men like George Wash-

---

[1]Melvin Lee Steadman, *Falls Church By Fence and Fireside* (Falls Church, Va.:
Falls Church Public Library, 1964), p. 1.

ington and George Mason, great patriots and statesmen, concerned themselves as well with problems of parish and community, and they played major roles in the early history of The Falls Church.

In the early days of Virginia the great rivers flowing from the Blue Ridge to Chesapeake Bay served as roads by which the early settlers moved into the wilderness to establish homes and later to ship out their crops and bring in goods. As the population passed the frontiers, new parishes and new counties were carved out of older ones. The part of Virginia known as the "Northern Neck" is the land lying between the Potomac and the Rappahanock Rivers. The land had been granted by King Charles II to some of his adherents, and before 1700 it had become the property of Lord Fairfax, whose agents sold the land to settlers. In 1730 Hamilton Parish was taken from Overwharton, and the following year Prince William County was established. Still later, in 1742, Fairfax County was formed from Prince William County. In 1757 Loudoun County was taken from Fairfax. The County of Alexandria, D.C., which is now Arlington, was ceded to the Federal Government in 1801. It was retroceded to Virginia in 1846. The City of Alexandria was incorporated in 1852, and nearly 100 years later in 1948 the town of Falls Church, named after "the church on the road to the Falls," became the City of Falls Church.

Melvin Steadman points out that at the time the church was founded there was "nothing in this area except plantations and small farms, and here and there an occasional Ordinary (tavern). The road to the Little Falls of the Potomac was intersected by the road from Alexandria to Leesburg, once known as Middle Turnpike, and now known as Leesburg Pike (Broad Street). It was at this crossroads about three miles distant that the Falls Church was built."[2]

To go back to the very earliest times, the individual colonial churches did not have ministers or vestries and the parish was often 40 to 50 miles in extent. The people of each new parish elected a Vestry, who selected a minister to serve the whole parish, and who built churches at different places as needed. In 1724 the minister of Overwharton Parish reported that he had one church and several chapels and about 650 families. One of these chapels was that known as Occoquan, situated about two miles north of that stream.

With the removal of the Indian menace the settlers turned their attention to their principal crop—tobacco. Early in the eighteenth century the area was comprised of gentry, indentures, and slaves. As the communities grew and flourished, the settlers established churches and schools and improved their government. The history of The Falls Church begins in Truro Parish.

---

[2]Ibid., p. 11

NEW TRURO PARISH ELECTS A VESTRY

In 1732 the General Assembly passed an act providing that Hamilton Parish be divided, the upper part to be known as Truro Parish, the lower part to remain Hamilton. The boundaries of Truro as then established were along the River Occoquan and Bull Run "thence to the Indian thoroughfare of the Blue Ridge" (now Ashby's Gap) then along the Blue Ridge to the Potomac, and down the Potomac to the Occoquan. This is the area of present-day Loudoun, Fairfax and Arlington Counties and the City of Alexandria. The Sheriff of Prince William County, as ordered in the law, called a meeting of "freeholders and housekeepers" in the Parish to elect 12 of the "most able and discreet persons to make up the Vestry." The election was held at the Occoquan Church, which had been built by Overwharton Parish prior to 1730. The first Vestry for Truro was held on November 7, 1732. Present were: Denis McCarty, John Heryford, Edward Barry, Charles Broadwater, Richard Osborn, John Lewis, Gabriel Adams, Edward Ems. "Having taken the oaths prescribed by law, and subscribed to be conformable to the doctrine and discipline of the Church of England," they elected Edward Barry as Clerk of the Vestry, and John Heryford and Edward Ems as Church Wardens, and instructed Barry to "provide proper books for the minutes and orders."

The Vestry was by law responsible for the administration of religion and the moral health of all people in the Parish. They must provide a minister, build and maintain churches, provide for the poor, the sick and orphans, make presentments to the County Court in adultery cases, appoint processioners to establish boundaries of patented lands, and levy a poll tax on all tithables to pay for these costs. All white males over 15 years and all Negro males and females over 15 were tithables. After being elected, they filled vacancies that occurred in their membership. The General Assembly provided for new vestry elections when dividing a parish and could do so at other times. The Bishop of London had spiritual authority over all the colonies, including the licensing of ministers and the sending of missionaries. Upon request of the Vestry the Royal Governor could "induct" a minister into a parish, after which he was irremovable except for cause. A minister's salary was set by law at 16,000 pounds of tobacco per year with the use of a glebe. (A glebe was a farm set aside for the use of the minister of a parish.) Tobacco was the cash crop, and it was inspected by County inspectors at warehouses to which every producer must bring it before offering it for sale. Taxes were levied and paid in tobacco.

At the second Vestry held March 26, 1733, the Church Wardens were ordered to advertise for bids on "the building of a church at the Cross Roads near Michael Reagans," and a Vestry on April 19 engaged the Rev. Lawrence DeButts to preach three times in each month for one year at "Occoquan Church, the new Church or Wm. Gunnels, and at the Chappel above Goose Creek" for 8000 pounds of tobacco.

CONTRACT LET FOR THE NEW (FALLS) CHURCH

Later the same year on June 9, the minutes for the Vestry of Truro Parish record the presence of: John Heryford, Edward Ems, Church Wardens; Denis McCarty, Wm. Godfrey, John Struman, Giles Tillett, Michael Ashford, Edward Barry and Gabriel Adams, Vestrymen. Also included is this order: "Whereas Mr. Richard Blackburn has this day agreed with this Vestry to build a church at the crossroads near Michael Reagans in this parish of the following dimensions, viz: 40 feet in length, 22 feet wide and 13 feet pitch, to be weather boarded, covered, and all the inside work performed and done after the same manner the work on Occoquan Church is done, for the sum of 33,500 pounds of tobacco. It is therefore ordered that one half of the said sum of 33,500 pounds of tobacco be levied for the said Blackburn at the laying of the parish levy and paid to him, or his order, by the collectors for this parish, as soon as the outside work of the said Church is finished, and that the remainder thereof be levied for him at the laying of the parish levy...in the year 1734... and it is further agreed to by the said Blackburn...to have the said Church covered and weather boarded by the last day of June...1734, and finished by the time of the last payment. *Ordered* that William Godfrey and Michael Ashford, two of the members of this Vestry take care that the work upon the church before mentioned be well and sufficiently done and performed."

Readers were appointed to the various churches to lead the people's responses and the singing. The Apostles' Creed, Ten Commandments and Lord's Prayer were painted on wooden plates on the wall. In those days few people had prayer books, and the reader conducted prayer services when the minister was not present. A Vestry on October 12, 1733 laid the first levy for Truro Parish (Appendix A) and appointed Joseph Johnson as the first Reader at The Falls Church and Goose Creek Chapel. Edward Barry, Vestry Clerk, served as Reader at the Occoquan Church.

A GLEBE BOUGHT

At a Vestry on June 4, 1734, a proposal was accepted from John Heryford to sell 300 Acres "Scituate, lying and being on Accotink" for a glebe, for 12,000 pounds, tobacco. In October a Vestry laid the levy. (Appendix A lists the levies laid each year and the Church

Wardens appointed for the ensuing year. The Vestry at levy time appointed one or two members to collect the tobacco which was paid out to the persons stipulated. Often the Wardens served as collectors. Usually a six percent fee was paid for collection.)

Among the items included in 1734 were:

To The Revd. Mr. DeButts, for preaching 8 sermons 1970
Iohn Masson, for keeping a house for the minister
    to preach in 530
Joseph Johnson, Reader at the Chappels 1300

Mr. DeButts had served from May 1733 to September 1734. Masson was paid for services at the Falls Church until the building was completed in the summer of 1734.

CHARLES GREEN RECOMMENDED AS MINISTER

At a Vestry on November 18, 1735, "Augustine Washington, gent., being this day sworn one of the members of this Vestry took his place therein." (Captain Washington was the father of George Washington.) The levy was laid at 7 lbs per poll. There had been no minister for the past year. Three readers received 1000 pounds of tobacco each for the services they had held in three churches and for the first time a sexton, Thomas Bennet, was paid at the Falls Church. At a Vestry on August 19, 1736, "Mr. Chas. Green being recommended. . .by Capt. Augustine Washington as a person qualified to officiate as a minister. . .as soon as he shall receive orders from his Grace the Bishop of London. . . It is ordered. . .that as soon as the said Green has qualified himself. . .he be received and entertained as minister of said Parish, and the. . .Vestry do humbly recommend. . .Charles Green to the Right Honorable Thomas, Lord Fairfax, for his letters of recommendation and presentation to his Grace the said Lord Bishop of London to qualify him."

The levy laid on October 11, 1736, included these items of particular interest.

To the Rev. James Keith..10.544 lbs
To Saml. Bronaugh for building a Vestry house
    and making seats at the Church, to be lodged
    in the hands of the Church Wardens and paid
    when the work is finished and not before 2500
To Rev. John Holmes in part of his next year's salary 5000

At that time the Vestry House was at Pohick Church. Mr. Keith had served for the past year, probably giving three Sundays a month to the three churches in Truro Parish. The Vestry also ordered that "the Rev. John Holmes be received and entertained in this Parish as minister thereof, and that he preach 6 times a year at Goose Creek, taking the time from the new (Falls) Church." (A note at the bottom of the minutes signed by Chas. Green, reads, "The levity of the members of the Vestry is worth noting. They applyd to Col. Colvill and entered an order 23, Sept. 1734 for him to procure a clergyman from England. By the order on the page they gave Chas. Green a title to the Psh. when ordained, and he had scarcely left the country when they received Mr. John Holmes. N.B. Mr. Holmes was an itinerant preacher without any orders and recd contrary to law." Apparently, Mr. Holmes did not stay long. The Rev. Joseph Blumfield served on a part-time basis from May to August 1737.

It is interesting to note the specifications for buildings on the glebe according to contract let to William Beverley by a Vestry on April 12, 1737. It specified a frame mansion house 24 feet square and 10 feet to the pitch with brick underpinning, a brick chimney at each end; a kitchen 16 feet by 20 feet, a barn 20 feet by 30 feet, as well as a dairy and a meat house, each 12 feet square. All were to be completed by October 1738 for 36,900 pounds of tobacco.

At this same meeting a contract was let concerning the Falls Church: "John Summers, having this day agreed with this Vestry to pail [enclose] in the yard about the *new church* after the same manner the yard about the Church at Pohick is pailed in, only the pails to be sawed, to make good and sufficient shutters for the windows of the said church, and to make and erect two good and substantial horse blocks at the church aforesaid for 3000 lbs. tobacco."

THE REV. CHARLES GREEN RECEIVED AS MINISTER

Having completed his studies, and been ordained in London, the Rev. Charles Green must have presented himself to Truro Parish, for the minutes of the Vestry held August 13, 1737, record: "And it now appearing to this Vestry as well by the letter of the Hon. William Gooch, Esq., Lt. Governor of Virginia, as the letter of the Rev. Mr. James Blair, Commissary, that the said Green is legally and regularly ordained, it is therefore ordered by this Vestry that said Greene be received into and entertained as minister of this parish, and that he be provided, as the laws of this colony direct. Ordered, that the Church Wardens place the people that are not already placed, in Pohick and the new churches, in pews, according to their several ranks and degrees. Ordered, that the Rev. Mr. Chas. Greene preach 4 times a year only at the Chappell above Goose Creek. And that the Sunday he preaches at the said Chappell the sermon shall be taken from the new church." This Vestry included Jeremiah Bronaugh and Thos. Lewis, Church Wardens; Denis McCarty, Augustine Washington (father of George), Richard Osborn, John Heryford, John Sturman, Edward Barry, Vestrymen. In the levy of 1738 the Vestry included 8000 lbs. tobacco to "buy ornaments for the churches and books for the Chappel and plate for communion."

FAIRFAX COUNTY ESTABLISHED

In December 1742 the new County of Fairfax was carved out of Prince William County. The new county encompassed the Parish of Truro. In 1743 the Vestry, on order of the County Court, provided for the processioning of lands in the Parish. ("To procession" is defined as a legal expression, meaning "to establish the bounds of a parish, lands, etc." and was in use in England and the Southeastern United States, especially Virginia.) The area was laid off in 18 precincts and two processioners were appointed for each to establish the boundaries of all land owners and report back "according to law."

The following year, in 1744 the General Assembly dissolved the Truro Vestry "at the Vestry House of Truro Parish. . .and the Sheriff. . .Wm. Payne, Gent., made returns that pursuant to the late act of the Assembly for dissolving the Vestry of this Parish he caused an election to be publicly had and made by the freeholders and housekeepers of said Parish who elected for Vestrymen. . .Capt. John West, Capt. Lewis Ellzey, Mr. John Sturman, Capt. John Minor, Mr. Hugh West, Mr. Andrew Hutchinson, Capt. Richard Osborn, Mr. Daniel French, Mr. Edward Ems, Mr. Robert Bogess, Col. John Colvill, Major Chas. Broadwater." It was this Vestry that "ordered that a gallery be built at the west end of the Upper (Falls) Church with 4 seats and rails and turned banisters." (The gallery was never built.) They further ordered that there be a reader at each church in this parish and that the minister. . .make choice of proper persons to officiate.

DEED FOR THE CHURCHYARD

The duties of the Reader or Clerk were important, and John Wybird Dainty became Clerk at the Falls Church in June 1745. It was ordered by the Vestry on Oct. 16, 1746, "that the Church Wardens do pay unto John Trammel. . .50 shillings for two acres of land at the Upper Church, and that Clerk do procure deeds for said Trammel to convey the same to this Parish."

With the completion of the Rocky Run Church, a structure 40 feet long, 22 feet wide and 13 foot pitch "after the manner of the Upper Church," there were four churches in Truro. Mr. Green was directed to "preach eight times in the year at the New Church," taking the time equally from the other three churches. Rocky Run was now the "New Church," and The Falls Church became the "Upper Church."

SEATS MADE FOR ALEXANDRIA CHURCH

That Vestry also "Ordered that the Church Wardens have seats made for the Church at Alexandria." This order and the allowance to Capt. West for "part of building the desk at Alexandria" are the only references in the Truro minutes to a levy or appropriation for building, furnishing or repairing a church at Alexandria, although a Clerk after 1753 and a Sexton after 1755 were regularly included in the levies. Some of the people in the new town provided the building rent free.

The levy of November 28, 1757 included:

"To John Lumley, Clerk at Falls Church
and Alexandria ....2000 lbs
"To.........Jno Wybird Dainty, to purchase clothes for him
to be laid out. P. Church Wardens ....500 lbs

This is the first use of "Falls Church" in the minutes. Since 1745 it had been the "Upper Church" and before that it was the "New Church." John W. Dainty served as Clerk at the Falls Church from 1745 to 1753, then moved to Alexandria, where he served until his death in 1756. His signature as a witness is on the deed to the church-yard of The Falls Church. The levy of 1758 included these Falls Church items:

To Gerard Trammel, charged a levy, tho' a patroller..............26 lbs
John Richards, seats at the (Upper) Falls Church ....150 lbs

TRURO DIVIDED . . . CAMERON FORMED

By this time there were 1745 tithables in Truro Parish, as compared with 681 in 1733. By act of the Assembly in October 1748, Truro Parish was divided again: "By Difficult Run. . .from the mouth to the head thereof. All above would be called Cameron Parish, all below would remain Truro." In the ensuing election the name of George Mason appears on the Vestry for the first time. Others elected for Truro were: Hugh West, James Hamilton, Chas. Broadwater, Daniel McCarty, Wm. Payne, Abraham Barnes, Thos. Wren, Robert Boggess, John Turley, Wm. Peake and Jeremiah Bronaugh. With this further division only the old Pohick Church and the Upper (Falls) Church were left in Truro Parish.

One of the first tasks of the new Vestry was to order "that an addition be built to the Upper Church according to a plan produced to the Vestry. And Charles Broadwater, Gent., undertakes to do the same and finish and compleat it by the laying of the next Parish levy" for 12,000 pounds of tobacco.

NEW GLEBE AND BUILDINGS

In 1751 the General Assembly authorized the sale of the glebe, and it was sold in 1752 for 50 pounds current money. The Vestry then purchased 176 acres adjacent to the old glebe from the Rev. Chas. Green for 13,500 lbs. tobacco. A later Vestry laid the levy and let the contract for the glebe buildings: "Mr. Thomas Waite undertakes to build the dwelling house and other buildings on the glebe according to an order of the Vestry of September 18, 1752 and a plan thereof offered by himself within 2 years for 425 pounds current money. . .in 2 payments and Mr. Chas. Green undertakes to do the rest of the buildings." The new dwelling house was to be of brick.

GREEN TO PREACH AT ALEXANDRIA

For a brief time services were held every Sunday at The Falls Church. The Clerk of the Upper Church (John Wybird Dainty) was ordered by a Vestry in October 1752 to read prayers every intervening Sunday and that he be allowed 1200 lbs. of tobacco per annum for his salary. He alternated with the Rev. Charles Green. However, at a Vestry on June 4, 1753, "On petition of Capt. John West the Revd. Mr. Charles Green was ordered to preach every third Sunday in the Town of Alexandria. The Vestry further ordered that year "that the Church Wardens agree with some workmen to make seats and horse blocks at the several churches in this parish." When next the Vestry met to lay the levy on November 27, 1754, the Hon. William Fairfax was appointed Vestryman to succeed Hugh West, deceased. Capt. John West was allowed 100 lbs tobacco for "part of building the desk at Alexandria."

GEORGE WASHINGTON, VESTRYMAN

At a Vestry held on October 25, 1762, the levy was laid and "Ordered that George Washington, Esq. be chosen and appointed one of the vestrymen of this Parish in the room of William Peake, gent. deceased." Colonel Washington took the required oaths at the Fairfax County Court House, on February 15, 1763, and attended his first Vestry which was held at the Falls Church. "At a Vestry for Truro Parish held at the Falls Church March 28, 1763. Present: Henry Gunnel, Wm. Payne, Jun. Church Wardens; John West, William Payne, Chas. Broadwater, Thos. Wren, Abraham Barnes, Danl. McCarty, Robert Boggess and George Washington, Gentlemen, Vestrymen, who being there met to examine into the state of the said church greatly in decay and want of repairs and likewise whether the same should be repaired or a new one built, and whether at the same place or removed to a more convenient one, and likewise to view the addition built by Mr. Charles Broadwater and what he hath been deficient in the work. *Resolved,* it is the opinion of this Vestry that the old Church is rotten and unfit for repair, but that a new Church be built at the same place. Resolved, that James Wren and Owen Williams do value the work to be done by Mr. Broadwater on the new addition, that is, the price of glazing 3 windows and plastering the said house, together with the materials necessary for the same and report to the next Vestry. Ordered, that the Clerk of the Vestry advertise in the Maryland and Virginia Gazettes for workmen to meet at the said church on the 29th of August next, if fair, if not on the next fair day, to undertake the building a brick church to contain 1600 square feet on the floor, with a suitable gallery and bring a plan of the church and price according to the same. Ordered, that the Church Wardens employ workmen to repair the windows on the north side and east end of the old church and repair the shutters of the new addition." There is no record of a meeting in August. Probably no workmen appeared.

The next Vestry was held October 3, 1763. They laid the levy, including 30,000 lbs. "towards building the Falls Church,". . ."Ordered that Geo. William Fairfax and George Washington Esq. be appointed Church Wardens for the ensuing year. Ordered that the Vestry meet at Alexandria the Third Monday in March next. . .to agree with workmen to undertake the building a church at or near the old Falls Church and that the Church Wardens advertise the same. . .for six weeks." Apparently no bidders showed up, but on March 20, 1764, the Wardens advertised again for bids to be received in June at The Falls Church. Again no bidders appeared. This was Washington's last official act connected with The Falls Church. At a Vestry on October 9, 1764, the levy was laid, including "For building churches in the Parish 20,000 lbs. tobacco."

TRURO DIVIDED AGAIN. FAIRFAX FORMED.

In November 1764, the House of Burgesses received a petition that the parish be divided. A bill introduced by the two Burgesses from Fairfax County, George Johnston and John West, was passed, and took effect in February 1765. This bill placed nearly all the Washington lands in the new Fairfax Parish, including Mt. Vernon, which was much nearer to the old Pohick Church. Vestry elections were held in March for both Truro and Fairfax Parishes. Washington was elected to the Fairfax Vestry, as was George Johnston. When the House of Burgesses met again in May, another petition praying a more equal division and several in opposition thereto, were read to the House and referred to the Committee on Grievances. A new bill was introduced and passed under which the boundary between the two parishes was moved north to Little Hunting Creek, which enters the Potomac above Mount Vernon. A second set of Vestry elections was held in July and this time Washington was elected to the Truro Vestry. The Falls Church and Alexandria became part of Fairfax Parish. Pohick Church was the one remaining church in

Truro Parish, but a second church was being planned south of present-day Fairfax.

In February 1765 the Rev. Charles Green died after nearly 28 years as minister in Truro Parish. He had practised medicine before ordination, and appears to have practised to some extent afterwards. The glebe was on the Accotink near Mt. Vernon, and Washington records in his diary on January 4, 1760, "Mrs. Washington seemed to be very ill. Wrote Dr. Green this afternoon, desiring his company to visit her in the morning. Sun. 5, Mrs. Washington appears to be something better. Mr. Green came to visit her at 11." Dr. Green became a large landowner and left 3000 acres to his wife. In his later years his health appears to have been poor, but the Vestry Minutes show that he missed only five meetings in 28 years. At the start of his ministry there were three churches. From 1746 until 1749 when Cameron County was separated there were four churches. After that only Pohick and The Falls Church remained in the parish until the Alexandria Church was started in 1753.

Early in his service, the Vestry had authorized a reader for *each* church to be chosen by him. For the last four years of his life he had only one reader to serve the three churches. Wet weather, muddy roads and high streams with no bridges kept both minister and people from attending at times. Church services were not held regularly, as today. In 1752 and part of 1753 The Falls Church had services every Sunday, every other one a prayer service read by a Clerk. From 1761 to 1764 with only one reader in the parish, services probably were held about two Sundays a month. (Appendix C lists the Readers [Clerks] and Sextons at the Falls Church.)

FAIRFAX VESTRY ORGANIZED

The second Fairfax Parish election was on July 20, 1765 and the first Vestry was held August 26, 1765. Present were John West, William Payne, Jr., John Dalton, Thomas Wren, William Adams, Edward Duling, Richard Sandford, Daniel French, Thomas Shaw and Townsend Dade. Major Charles Broadwater and Edward Blackburn, also elected, were absent. West, Payne, Broadwater, Wren and French had served on the Truro Vestry. John Minor was elected Clerk of the Vestry. A Committee was appointed to apply to Truro for the part due the new parish of the 50,000 lbs. of tobacco levied, "for building new churches," and for the share of the value of the glebe and communion plate of Truro. Committees were also appointed to "take care of the Poor" and "look after repairs to the church" until the first levy. Dalton was authorized to buy a bible and 2 prayer books for the Lower (Alexandria) Church. A Vestry on November 20 laid the levy, including 31,185 for "building new churches." Payne and Dalton were appointed Church Wardens for the ensuing year. Report was received that 26,676 lbs. of tobacco was due from Truro out of the amount levied last year. The Wardens were *ordered* to "take care of the poor" and "agree with a doctor to attend the sick."

THE REV. TOWNSEND DADE RECEIVED

At a Vestry on December 30, 1765, "the Rev. Townsend Dade, Jr. presented his credentials as a minister of the Church of England and offered his services as incumbent for this Parish and as such he is received." Thos. Wren was appointed Clerk, and Gerard Trammel Sexton at The Falls Church. The Wardens were ordered "to advertise the want of a glebe" and the "want of a Vestry House at the Falls Church." The Truro Vestry house had been built at Pohick Church in 1736. Now one would be needed for the new parish of Fairfax.

VESTRY HOUSE AT THE FALLS CHURCH

At a Vestry, March 17, 1766, contract was let to Henry Darne to build the Vestry House for 2500 lbs. tobacco. The specifications are in Appendix D. At a Vestry on September 25, 1766, ". . .the said Vestry house has been builded and received," the Wardens were ordered to pay Darne, and also "ordered that he be paid 810 lbs transfer tobacco for planking and securing the windows in the church and making a horse block."

At a Vestry held October 16, 1766, Adams and Dalton were appointed Church Wardens "for the ensuing year," and "Ordered the advertisement of the building of a church at The Falls Church 2400 square feet from outside to outside for the walls to be raised to admit of galleries," the work "to be let the first Monday in March next ensuing." They also ordered the advertisement of the glebe for the same date. A Vestry held November 15, appointed James Wren as Vestryman "in place of Edward Blackburn resigned." A Vestry on November 27 laid the levy, including 31,125 lbs. of tobacco "for Building Churches." They also speeded up the building program. "Ordered, that the Church wardens advertise the building of two churches 2400 feet square each to be built of brick from outside to outside and the walls to be raised to admit of galleries, on the first day of January next, if fair, if not on the next fair day, one of the churches |to be| where the old Falls Church stands and the other at Alexandria, the undertakers to meet at The Falls Church and bring in their plans."

CONTRACTS LET FOR TWO BRICK CHURCHES

In accordance with the advertisement, James Wren, who lived in a house on Shreve Road which is still standing, submitted a plan and a proposal to build The Falls Church. Mr. Wren had been appointed to the Vestry six weeks earlier. The Wren family claim descent from Sir Christopher Wren, according to Melvin Steadman in his *Falls Church By Fence and Fireside*. The minutes for a Vestry on January 1, 1767, state: "Conforming to an order of the Vestry 27 November last directing the Church Wardens to publish the letting out of two churches to the lowest bidders, that is to say, one at or near The Falls Church, the other at Alexandria, the Vestry have met to receive their plans. James Wren produced a plan 60 feet by 40 feet which was made choise of and agreed to build the same for 599 pounds and 15 shillings. The proposals for payment to be made as follows: that is to say 250 pounds to each by the end of October next ensuing in the year 1768, 140 pounds to each in the year 1769, 140 pounds to each in the year 1770 and the balance. James Parsons agrees to build the church at Alexandria agreeable to the plan produced by James Wren for 600 pounds currency." Attached to the minutes were "The Specifications for the Churches." (Appendix E) The Vestry further "*Ordered* that the Church Wardens apply to the Clerk of Prince William for an abstract of the deed relative to land at and adjoining The Falls Church. They also requested the Church Wardens to "take bond and security of James Wren and James Parsons on or before the first day of March next ensuing," and James Wren received 40 shillings for the use of his plan and bill of scantling.

Members of the congregation at the Alexandria Church apparently felt they needed a larger church as the minutes of a Vestry in May 1767 indicate that a petition was received for an addition of 10 feet to the Church being built at Alexandria. We read, "It is agreed that they make such addition agreeable to their contract with Mr. James Parsons, the present undertaker, who has agreed to build the said church and lay off the pews by a plan produced and numbered. . . which pews are to be sold by the said James Parsons for his benefit, but with this exception that no one is permitted to be a purchaser but inhabitants of this parish or those that pay taxes in the same."

During 1767 James Wren must have been engaged in brick making. The bricks were made of clay dug, mixed, molded and burned nearby. Dr. Joseph Packard in his *Recollections of a Long Life* writes, "I used to visit an old woman near Falls Church. She was over ninety when she died, and remembered the kiln where the bricks for The Falls Church were made, and had played in it as a child." The kiln, according to Mr. Nathan Lynch, whose uncle, William Lynch, was sexton for many years before 1861, was located about 300 yards west of the church on the old Fairfax Road. Traces of the clay pits were visible in 1940.

Col. Wren was ordered by a Vestry on February 8, 1768, "to fix the church as near to the northside of the old church so that it fronts directly south." The Vestry evidently kept an eye on construction on the new church building as it progressed, for the minutes of April 19 order that "Major Broadwater, Mr. Payne and Mr. Adams do inspect the work of the upper church to be built by Mr. James Wren, undertaker, as often as they shall think necessary, and if they see cause to call a Vestry that they have a survey, they order the same." A similar order appointed Capt. West, Mr. Shaw and Capt. Dalton to look after the Alexandria Church. "Ordered that the Church Wardens pay the undertakers the balance of their first years payment as fast as it comes to their hands." A July 30 Vestry ordered the Wardens to sell "all the tobacco in their hands for the best price" they could get.

On October 6, the Vestry met to inquire into the conduct of the Reverend Townsend Dade. After discussion it was voted 6 to 5 to take no notice of the matter.

BRICK CHIMNEY BUILT IN VESTRY HOUSE

A Vestry on November 29, 1768, laid the levy, and included 28,-784 lbs. tobacco "for building churches," and "To James Wren per acct. for moving and building the chimney in the Vestry House with brick—19 pds. 17s. 4d." The remains of this chimney foundation were found under the roots of a tree about 160 years old, which was cut down in 1959 to make room for the new parish house. The location of this tree is shown on the plans for the 1952 Parish Hall. It was under the choir vesting room, near the east side of the original lot purchased for the first church.

As work progressed on the new church, the Wardens were ordered on November 29, 1768 to "advance to Mr. James Wren, one of the undertakers for building the church at the Falls, 50,000 pounds of tobacco towards his payment to be made in the year 1769 and at the same time give bond that in case of the purchase of a glebe and money is wanting that he is to pay it upon demand. It is further ordered that the collector pay Mr. James Wren three thousand pounds of tobacco under the payment to be made in the year 1769."

The same Vestry appointed Daniel French and Thomas Shaw as Church Wardens during this critical time of construction. Col. West was "ordered to apply to Mr. John Alexander of Stafford for deeds for one acre of land near Alexandria which the church is erected upon." In addition, Charles Broadwater, John West and William Payne, or any two of them, were ordered to "apply to the Vestry of

Truro to settle and receive the sums due this parish and to pay the same into the hands of the Church Wardens."

The Vestry held July 24. 1769. received a report from Major Broadwater and Mr. Duling on their receipts and disbursements for church construction. Both Wren and Parsons had received their full payments of 250 pounds currency for the first year and 140 pounds for the second year. Earlier. Wren had received two pounds currency for his design.

The new Falls Church must have been completed by late fall for we find that a Vestry on November 28. 1769. laid a levy. which included "19,996 lbs. tobacco for Public Services" which could be used towards paying the balances yet due on the churches or for buying a glebe. James Wren was also reimbursed for stone steps (2 pounds 12 sh.) and "extraordinary work on the windows (6 pounds 15 sh.)." The stone steps are shown in the 1862 Brady photographs. James Wren and Townsend Dade. Sr.. were appointed Church Wardens for the ensuing year.

THE BRICK FALLS CHURCH ACCEPTED BY VESTRY

At a Vestry held on December 20. 1769. "It is agreed that Mr. James Wren has completed the work at The Falls Church agreeable to the contract and that his bond be delivered to him. and that they have received the same for the use of the parish. *Ordered* that James Wren and Townsend Dade. Church Wardens. do allot seats for the parishioners according to dignity. It is *ordered* that the old church be sold immediately. as to be removed by the last of February. a distance sufficient from the new building. and the purchaser to give bond and security payable next June come 12 months. and if it is not removed by that time that the property be vested in the parish again. *Ordered*. that John Brawner give bond and security immediately to the present church wardens for 7 pounds 5 shillings. the amount the old church sold for. It is agreed by the Vestry. at the expense of Mr. William Payne that James Wren fix a seat upon the upper platform for the benefit of his wife. *Ordered*. that James Wren and William Adams are appointed Collectors for this parish. *Ordered*. that the Church Wardens pay James Wren 30 pounds in currency in part payment of what is due him from the parish. *Ordered*. that the Church Wardens advertise the want of a glebe and those desiring to sell make application to them." The Vestrymen present at the meeting when the present Falls Church was accepted were: William Payne. William Adams. John Dalton. Charles Broadwater. Edward Duling. Thomas Shaw. Richard Sandford. Daniel French. Henry Gunnel. James Wren. C.W.. and Townsend Dade. C.W.

Colonel George Washington records in his diary in March 1770,

"By Mr. Wm. Adams for my subscription to decorating The Falls Church—1 pound."

The worthy Mr. Wren submitted an account of eight pounds currency to the Vestry" for writing the commandments and making a table for the communion" in May 1770. These plates of the Commandments were intended for the use of The Falls Church since table for the communion" in May 1770. These plates of the *Commandments* were intended for the use of The Falls Church since the church at Alexandria was not completed until 1773. It is not known what happened to the communion table. The Commandments, according to one account, were carried off to a church in Hartford, Connecticut, in 1862.

In its search for glebe lands the Vestry met with Daniel Jennings on May 27, 1770, and agreed to take his land "supposed to be about 400 and more acres for a glebe, paying 15 shillings per acre." A survey reported that fall showed about 515 acres. The site of the farm was north of Glebe Road, between Lee Highway and North Washington Boulevard. At a Vestry held November 26, 1770, the levy was set at 50 lbs. per poll. Another Vestry held December 17 reported: "On finding a further sum was wanting for the payment of the glebe, then already layed it is ordered that the sum of 10,000 pounds of tobacco be added to the sum already laid." The levy thus was "To 1248 tythables at 59 tobacco per poll—73,360 [lbs.]."

It is interesting to note that a year later on November 25, 1771, a Vestry "Ordered that John West receive the rents due from the glebe land and to tenant them as he shall see necessary." It was also "ordered that the Church Wardens agree with some person or persons to take care of the poor and hire a house if necessary for their reception." The sexton at Alexandria at the same Vestry was ordered "to fix the mode of corpses burying. . .and that they be buried at least 6 feet deep."

ALEXANDRIA CHURCH ACCEPTED

The records show that a Vestry was held at Alexandria on May 25, 1772, to inspect progress on the church building. James Parsons was present and gave no satisfactory reply as to completion, whereupon the Vestry "ordered the Wardens to advertise its finishing" for Monday, June 8. "At a Vestry held at the church nigh Alexandria on June 8, 1772," the minutes state, "contract was let to John Carlyle for finishing the work at 220 pounds currency, by December 25th next."

Upon completion of the Alexandria Church a Vestry held February 29, 1773, received "the church at Alexandria from the undertaker, John Carlyle," and "ordered, that Wm. Copein and Joseph Gound do view the stone steps at the Alexandria church doors and report the value of them." The Vestry then sold the 10 pews by auction for a total of 298 pounds 10 shillings. The high bidder was George Washington at 36 pounds 10 shillings. Purchasers were inhabitants of the parish or taxpayers. Colonel Washington lived in Truro Parish, but he was also a taxpayer in Fairfax. These pews were sold to cover the cost of widening the church by ten feet, as previously agreed.

CONTRACT LET FOR GLEBE BUILDINGS

Following the purchase of a glebe, it was necessary to erect a Glebe House. The minutes of the Vestry for March 15, 1773, are illuminating.

"Ordered that the Church Wardens advertise the letting of a Glebe House 42 by 28...of brick the walls to be 19 feet from the bottom of cellar." The plan was to be produced at the letting and at the same time the necessary farm buildings were to be let. Bids were received on May 24, 1773, and a contract was awarded to Benjamin Ray to construct the glebe buildings for 653 pounds. This included the brick house and frame buildings which were: a 20 by 16 foot stable, a house of offices [toilet], with proper seats, and a log corn house. The work was to be completed by November 1775. An advance payment of 200 pounds was made: 140 pounds more to be payable in September and 102 pounds in December following. "The above payments to be maid in common currency, that is dollars to six shillings, and half joes in proportion." (The dollar was a Spanish coin, having about one and one half times the silver content of the later dollar.)

A Vestry on November 6, 1773, laid the levy and included items of special interest:

"To James Wren for his plan of the Glebe House..........2 p. 10 s.

To Wm. Parkerson for his plan of the Glebe House ....1 p. 10 s."

A report of expenditures by the Church Wardens included:

"To Mr. Herbert for a bible and two prayer books for

The Falls Church...5 p. 16 s."

They also reported 201 p. 17 s. 7 d. received from Truro for the Fairfax share of the money from the sale of the glebe and communion plate.

As war clouds began to gather over the Colonies, the effect on prices and daily life in Virginia becomes evident. Following the closing of the port of Boston by Parliament on June 1, 1774, a Vestry held August 17, "Ordered that the Church Wardens sell the parish tobacco in their hands for the best price they can get either at public or private sale and be answerable to the Vestry for the same."

In June 1774 the colonial Governor Dunmore had dissolved the House of Burgesses. The First Continental Congress was called to meet in Philadelphia in September. George Washington was one of five delegates from Virginia. The next spring the Virginia Convention met on March 25, and Washington and Broadwater represented Fairfax County. The war clouds broke and the Revolutionary War began in April 1775 when the British soldiers met the Massachusetts militia at Lexington and Concord. The Second Continental Congress met in Philadelphia on May 25.

Despite the ominous rumblings daily life went on. On November 24, 1774, levy day, the Vestry "Ordered that James Wren do such things as he shall see necessary to the spring at The Falls Church."

A Vestry held February 20, 1775, with nine members present, ordered Gunnel to collect the levy, and they appointed Wren, Adams, Payne and Duling as committee to "view the glebe work." The Vestry appeared to be satisfied with the work because the minutes of a Vestry held at the glebe on June 16 report "having viewed the buildings at the glebe are of opinion that Benjamin, William and James Ray have performed everything. . .in a workmanlike manner and therefore the Vestry do hereby receive the said buildings." They also ordered the Church Wardens to pay the balance due on "Monday next, provided they have so much money in their hands." Notoriously delinquent in his attendance at Vestry meetings, the Rev. Townsend Dade was present at this one.

Meanwhile, the Continental Congress appointed Gen. George Washington as Commander-in-Chief of the Continental Army on June 15. On June 17 the Battle of Bunker Hill was fought. And so war came to the American colonies.

The only other Vestry held in 1775 laid the smallest levy in many years, 20 lbs. per poll, and directed the Wardens to "discharge the several cash debts this year assessed, in dollars, silver or paper at 6 shillings, half johannes of 9 pennyweight at 48 shillings. English guineas at 28 shillings, Spanish pistoles of 4 pennyweight 6 grains at 22 shillings."

A Vestry on April 15, 1776, with Charles Broadwater and John West, Jr., present, appointed Francis Adams as Collector at 10 percent, ordered the Wardens to pay two small bills, filed a bond and adjourned.

On May 15 the Virginia Convention, with Charles Broadwater and John West, Jr., representing Fairfax County, voted unanimously to instruct its delegates to the Continental Congress to propose a Declaration of Independence, which was passed on July 4, and also appointed a Committee to prepare a plan of government for Virginia.

VIRGINIA A COMMONWEALTH

The first General Assembly under the government of Virginia met in October 1776. Among the first acts was one entitled "An act for exempting the different Societies of Dissenters from contributing to the support and maintenance of the *church as by law established."* One section of the bill repealed all Acts of Parliament against dissenters, a second exempted dissenters from all levies and taxes for the support of the church and its ministers. The responsibilities of the Vestries remained unchanged, except that their authority to levy any tobacco for salaries of clergy, lay readers, and sextons, and for the building and repair of churches was suspended after January 1, 1777, except for commitments made prior to that date. Another section of the Act provided that for all time glebes already purchased, churches and chapels already built, all books, plate and ornaments, as well as private donations already made to each parish be reserved for the use of the church.

LAST LEVY INCLUDING SUPPORT OF THE CHURCH

"At a Vestry held at the Vestry House (Falls Church) on March 24, 1777, Present, Henry Gunnel, Wm. Payne, Richard Conway, Henry Darne, John Hunter, Richard Sandford, Chas. Broadwater, and James Wren," the minutes state that in accordance with the new law, payments were added for the Minister, for Elisha Powell as reader, Trammel as Sexton at the Falls, Edwards as Sexton at Alexandria, up to January 1, 1777. These, added to the estimates of November 23, made a total levy adopted of 48,750 pounds of tobacco. "John Scale is appointed Clerk of the Vestry in the room of John Hunter who is chosen as a Vestryman." At a Vestry held at the Vestry House, March 31, 1777, "John Muir is appointed to collect for this parish. Ordered that he receive 39 lbs. of tobacco for each tythable person in this parish, and in case of failure that he levy the same by distress." This was the last levy laid for the support of the Church but small items appear in later levies, for costs incurred prior to January 1, 1777.

The Vestry continued to be concerned with the poor of the parish, and the Vestry minutes for August 20, 1777, "Ordered that the Church Wardens pay Joseph Marle 24 pounds cash as an apprentice fee for Benjamin Watson. Ordered that Francis Summers employ the parishioners under his care in anything that he may think them capable of doing and render an account. . .at the laying of the next levy, and in case they disobey Mr. Summers he has full authority to deal with them as the law directs." (Mr. Summers provided a house to take care of the poor, probably in the Falls Church area.)

The war had not yet reached the South, but it was coming. Gen. Burgoyne surrendered at Saratoga, N.Y., on September 11, and the British captured Philadelphia on September 26, 1777. Congress fled to Lancaster, Pennsylvania.

REV. TOWNSEND DADE INVESTIGATED

It had been apparent for some time that the Rev. Townsend Dade was not carrying out his duties as a minister of the parish. A committee of the Vestry was ordered to wait upon him to learn "why he neglects his duty as a minister in the churches of this parish." Although his salary had stopped on January 1, he still occupied a fine glebe house with 500 acres. Becoming increasingly exasperated, the Vestry on November 24, 1777, ordered a Committee of eight members to "wait upon the Rev. Townsend Dade...to know whether he will resign the glebe as he fails to do his duty as a minister." It was reported that "the gentlemen appointed met at the Rev. Mr. Dade's and then and there the said Dade entered into a bond with the said Vestrymen for his appearance on this day (December 8, 1777) at the Vestry House, which he the said Dade has done, and has entered into another bond for his faithful performance as a minister and other purposes therein mentioned."

Apparently, the offending minister did not fulfill his promises because it is recorded in the minutes of a Vestry held February 28, 1778, that "In consequences of a meeting of the Vestry as to inquiring of the same Dade, Minister whether he would relinquish the glebe to the Vestry agreeable to his bond...and he refusing, it is *Ordered* that the said bond be put in force and that witnesses be summoned ...before two Justices of the Peace in...Alexandria on the third Monday in March next at the home of Adam Lynn, and that the said Dade have notice of the time and place of the meeting."

Things came to a head with a Vestry on June 7, 1778, which "ordered that the Rev. Townsend Dade's resignation of his rectory and parsonage be received and recorded. Ordered that Wm. Payne, Charles Conway and Charles Broadwater [vestrymen] immediately take possession of the glebe of this parish...and contracts for the tenants thereon for the rents that shall become due at the expiration of the year. Ordered that the Church Wardens of this Parish advertise in the Virginia and Maryland Gazettes, the vacancy of this parish in order to secure a minister for it." Later that year, the Rev. William West was selected and the Wardens directed to notify him.

During this trying period at The Falls Church the British abandoned Philadelphia in May 1778, and General Washington attacked them on their retreat at Monmouth. Late in July, the British crossed the Hudson to New York. In addition, new allies came to the aid of the American colonists with the entrance of France into the war. The French fleet was off New York.

The Wardens presented a letter of acceptance from the Rev. Mr. West, who promised to arrive by the end of November at a Vestry on October, 26. At this same Vestry an item of 7 pounds 4 sh. for "at-

20

tending Vestries" and for the first time 6 pounds "for mending graves" was given to Gerard Trammel. sexton.

THE REV. DAVID GRIFFITH RECEIVED AS MINISTER

The Rev. Mr. West enjoyed a short tenure as minister at The Falls Church apparently for a Vestry at the Vestry House at The Falls Church records on February 17, 1779, that the Rev. David Griffith had applied to be received as minister of the parish. We read, "Being unanimously chosen, it is ordered that the Church Wardens put him in possession of the glebe of this parish." Mr. Griffith had been minister of Shelburne Parish but resigned in May 1776 to enter the Continental Army as Chaplain of the 3rd Virginia Regiment. He had been a physician in New York before he went to England, where he was ordained in 1770. He came to Virginia in 1771. In a letter to his wife dated September 23, 1778, he writes of a letter from Captain Conway, a vestryman, concerning the vacancy. "There is a very fine glebe belonging to it. He mentions no salary only that he thinks a very genteel subscription will be made up." He resigned as Chaplain on March 18, 1779, and came to Fairfax Parish, where he served until his death in 1789.

PRICES SKY HIGH

The next Vestry held November 10, 1779, received Mr. Payne's accounts of receipts and disbursements, as Collector for 1777 and 1778. They laid a levy for the support of the poor and appointed John Parke Custis as Vestryman in place of Richard Sandford, resigned. Custis was the son of Martha Washington.

A Vestry on November 29, 1779, received further reports from Mr. Payne of receipts and disbursements for the poor, most of them recorded in the depreciated Continental Currency. Examples:

To 6 yds linen for Jane Russel at 48 shillings ....14 p. 8s. - 0
To 1 pr. shoes for Newton .... 6 p. 0s. - 0
To my trouble in furnishing Falls Church
with elements ....14 p. 0s. - 0

He sold 7,085 lbs. tobacco for 22 p. 10 s. 0 per 100 lbs. In 1770 the tobacco had sold at 20 shillings per 100 lbs., now it was 450 shillings. At this meeting some 15 indentures binding 17 orphan children were filed. In a four-year period prior to the war, these had ranged from four to six annually. Inevitably, the war had increased the number of orphans and the needs of the poor.

The Reverend Francis Asbury (Methodist) noted in his diary, May 4, 1780: "Preached at the Chapel in Fairfax and met Mr. Griffith, an Episcopal minister, who was friendly and we spent the afternoon together." The Methodist Chapel was in the present-day Oakwood Cemetery area.

THE WAR REACHES THE SOUTH

As history tells us, the British finally carried the war to the South. In May 1780 Charleston, S.C., surrendered, and General Gates was badly defeated at Camden in August. Virginia was not immune, for in January 1781 Benedict Arnold, now a British general, landed near Richmond and burned a foundry. In April a British warship carried off 16 Negroes from Mt. Vernon. The war had come to Virginia. Tarleton raided Charlottesville, forcing Governor Jefferson and the Legislature to flee across the Blue Ridge. The fortunes of war had begun to change, however. On September 5, 1781, a French fleet blocked the British fleet at the mouth of the Chesapeake Bay. Meanwhile, American and French troops were moving South. When General Cornwallis surrendered to General Washington on October 19 at Yorktown, Va., the Revolutionary War came to an end.

GALLERIES AUTHORIZED IN ALEXANDRIA CHURCH

One of the problems which faced the Vestry during and after the war was the inevitable war-time inflation. The Vestry took subscriptions for Mr. Griffith's salary payable in tobacco, and they also paid him for his services as a physician to the poor of the parish out of the levies from 1780 to 1782. The minutes in 1780 record the value of his subscription tobacco at 40 pounds currency, but in 1782 it had dropped to 15 shillings per hundredweight. The Continental currency was devalued, and every 40 pounds currency became one pound in the new currency. Payments to Francis Summers for the care of the poor in 1780 were reported at 2236 pounds currency, and in 1781 at 2826 pounds.

A Vestry of November 27, 1783, records the following: "Francis Summers will no longer board the poor. It is agreed by the Vestry that Robert Lindsay take care of all the poor committed to his charge to find them sufficient meat and drink and house room and fire fitting for their station and . . . is to be allowed 700 lbs. of transfer tobacco per year for every person sent to him." The 700 lb. allowance is well above the average of the 15 individual allowances listed for the past year. "James Wren and William Brown are appointed Church Wardens for the ensuing year. Wm. Brown is appointed Doctor for the poore for the parish." A bit further on is this statement: "Upon motion of the Rev. David Griffith, Wm. Brown, Wm. Herbert, Geo. Gilpin, Chas. Alexander, and Robert T. Hooe for leave . . . to erect galleries in the church of Fairfax Parish at Alexandria . . . applicants and all subscribers have leave to forward such designs . . . that the pews . . . built be the property of the subscribers, that they have leave to sell for reimbursement . . . the over plus . . . to be held by them for the uses of the same church . . . in repairing . . . Said galleries and pews . . . and to the repairs and uses of the said church . . . Ordered that they will build the galleries in such manner as not to stop the light flowing through the windows, and that whatever is taken up by the staircases below shall be given gratis in pews in the galleries." The Vestry agreed to the plan and gave the applicants leave to proceed as soon as they please. The galleries were completed in August 1787.

In February 1784, George Washington resigned as a Vestryman of Truro Parish, a position he had held since 1763. Since 1775 he had been almost continuously away from home.

DISESTABLISHMENT OF THE CHURCH

Reference is made repeatedly to the Disestablishment of the Church. This term is defined as the "depriving a church of its rights, position or privileges as an established church; withdrawing a church from its connection with the state." In 1784 the State Legislature completed the disestablishment of the Church. The act relieved the Vestries of all responsibility for the poor and orphans and provided for the election of two overseers of the poor every three years to assume these duties. The act also provided that the "Minister and Vestry" of each parish should be a corporation to have, hold, use and enjoy all glebes, churches, chapels, burying grounds, books, plate and ornaments then owned. It also provided for the future election of Vestries by members of the Church.

The last meeting of the old Colonial Vestry elected in 1765 was held at the Vestry House at the Falls Church on March 17, 1785. Of those elected in 1765 only Charles Broadwater remained. Final reports were made, and the remaining balance of 13 pounds, 18 shillings, 11 pence was appropriated to the needs of the poor at the discretion of the Church Wardens. It is interesting to note that provisions were made for paying the sexton, Gerard Trammell, at this final meeting of the Colonial Vestry. He had served faithfully since his appointment in 1759.

Thus, an era in the history of the Falls Church came to an end. Many dedicated men served the church in various capacities from the early days of the eighteenth century until close to the dawn of the nineteenth century. For a period of fifty years divine services were held more or less continuously at the church "on the road to Little Falls." Men like George Mason and George Washington sacrificed their time and comfort to attend Vestry meetings despite muddy roads, swollen streams and other inconveniences. They saw to it that the poor and indigent were taken care of, that the orphans were given homes and taught trades and that other temporal affairs of the church were carried out.

After the final disestablishment of the established church in Virginia the individual vestries were elected by members of the church. It is noteworthy that the Fairfax Parish Vestry enjoyed representation at the First Convention of the Protestant Episcopal Church in Virginia in Richmond in May 1785. Later, at the First General Convention of the Protestant Episcopal Church in the United States held at Christ Church, Philadelphia, in September 1785, the Reverend David Griffith was unanimously elected secretary.

THE PROTESTANT EPISCOPAL CHURCH BEGINS

"At an election of a Vestry for Fairfax Parish at the Vestry House on Easter Monday, 28th of March 1785, agreeable to the act of incorporation of the Protestant Episcopal Church, we the subscribers being appointed judges by a majority of the people present, do declare the under mentioned were duly elected by the following number of votes, viz.: Charles Broadwater 48, William Payne 48, James Wren 45, Robert Powell 45, Wm. Herbert 44, Robert T. Hooe 45, William Brown 36, George Gilpin 43, Dr. John Courts 43, Bryan Fairfax 41, John Hunter 35, Thomas West 25. Given under our hands the day and year above,

R. T. Hooe, Wm. Payne — C. W. 's

"At a meeting of the Corporation of the Minister and Vestry of the Protestant Episcopal Church in Fairfax Parish at the Vestry House 28th March 1785. Present the Revd. David Griffith," and the Vestrymen elect, of whom the first three were from The Falls Church area. "Mr. Bryan Fairfax is appointed by the unanimous vote of the corporation to represent the parish in convention together with the Rev. Mr. Griffith. Robert T. Hooe and William Payne are appointed Church Wardens for the ensuing year. Ordered that the Clerk of the late Vestry deliver to the Church Wardens all papers, minute books and records belonging to the parish which he has in his custody.

R.T. Hooe, Wm. Payne—C. Wns.

We the subscribers, this day elected Vestrymen for Fairfax Parish do declare that we will conform to Doctrine, Discipline and Worship of the Protestant Episcopal Church. Vestry House, 28 March 1785."

(Signed by the 12 Vestrymen)

FIRST CONVENTIONS

The First Convention of the Protestant Episcopal Church in Virginia was held in Richmond on May 18, 1785, the Reverend Mr. Griffith and Mr. Bryan Fairfax representing Fairfax Parish. There were present 36 clergymen and 71 laymen representing 69 parishes. In 1774 there had been 95 parishes, having 164 churches. The First

General Convention of the Protestant Episcopal Church in the United States met in Philadelphia on Sept. 28. 1785.

SUBSCRIPTIONS ASKED FROM MEMBERS

The Vestry of Fairfax Parish, meeting in March 1786, decided to send out a subscription list to all members in the parish, asking for financial support for the minister and "other contingent" expenses. In August they followed with a call for another subscription to cover the expenses of consecrating a bishop, the Reverend Mr. Griffith having been elected Bishop in the State Diocesan Convention of that year. At this meeting they also "Resolved that in the future collections shall be made at each church in this parish by the Church Wardens or Vestrymen present for the expenses of this church." This was the origin of the present-day custom of taking a collection at each service.

In August 1787 another Vestry election was held. Thomas West, William Lyles and David Stewart replaced Courts, Bryan Fairfax and Hunter in all vestry. The other nine were reelected. The General Assembly had repealed the 1784 law making the "Minister and Vestry" a corporation and voted instead for the election of Trustees to hold title to the property. The new Vestry meeting ten days later elected Oliver Price as Clerk at Alexandria and William Carlin, Clerk at The Falls Church at 7 pounds 15 shillings per year, and it set Mr. Griffith's salary at "not exceeding 750 pounds currency."

Sometime after 1786 Mr. Bryan Fairfax resigned as Vestryman. He was an ardent Royalist before the Revolution, according to the records. He was the son of William Fairfax of Belvoir, and he was ordained in 1786 by Bishop Samuel Seabury. During the period from 1790 to 1792 he served as rector of Fairfax Parish. Fairfax was confirmed as the eighth Lord Fairfax by the English House of Lords in 1800. His tombstone in Ivy Hill Cemetery, Alexandria, reads as follows: 'In memoriam—Right Hon. and Reverend Bryan, Lord Fairfax, Baron of Cameron, Rector of Fairfax Parish, Died at Mount Eagle August 7th, 1802, aged 65 years.' "[3]

Unfortunately the Rev. Mr. Griffith was forced to resign his election as Bishop in the spring of 1789. The Church in Virginia had never raised the money to send him to England for consecration. He attended the General Convention in Philadelphia in July and died there August 3, 1789. The records show that he served as minister of Fairfax Parish from 1779 to 1789.

---

[3]*Ibid.* p. 25.

THE REV. BRYAN FAIRFAX INDUCTED AS MINISTER

A Vestry was held March 15, 1790. Present, Brown, and Payne, Church Wardens, Herbert, Gilpin, West, Hooe, Conway and Stewart; Vestrymen. "James Wren and Richard Conway, gentlemen, subscribed to be conformable to the doctrine, discipline and worship of the Protestant Episcopal Church. The Rev. Bryan Fairfax has been inducted Minister of this Parish by an unanimous voice. *Ordered,* that the annual rents of the pews in the Church at Alexandria be lowered. . .those that rented at 5 pounds per annum in 1788 to be $10., those at 4 pounds to be $8. . .those at 3 pounds to be $6. . .Ordered, that the delinquent pews in the gallery, No. 8, No. 9, No. 10 and No. 11 be at the disposal of Dr. Wm. Brown, and the benefits arising from them until his is reimbursed the money he advanced for the erection of the gallery, amounting to 27 pounds 7 shillings and 10 pence, half penny with interest from 1787 until paid, after which they are to revert to the use and disposal of the Vestry. Ordered that it is the sense of this Vestry that the Glebe lands shall not be subjected to waste or let out to sub-tenants but that the Minister only shall occupy them, or rent them only to one tenant, whom he may choose. Adjourned without day, the new election being so near at hand."

The third Vestry election was held at The Falls Church on Easter Monday, April 5, 1790. At a meeting held the following month the Wardens were ordered to pay William Carlin, Reader at The Falls Church 7 pounds 10 shillings, and Gerard Trammel, Sexton, 3 pounds for yearly services due "last August."

During this period in which the Rev. Bryan Fairfax served as minister the Vestry met on April 10, 1791, and "did certify that there are 2 houses of worship belonging to the parish in good repair, that the parish has no personal property, that there is a glebe, containing 516 acres with a good brick building or dwelling house and outhouses thereon, and that the value thereof is probably 1000 pounds current money, that the Rev. Bryan Fairfax is appointed minister of this parish and at present officiates without any assistant minister and that they have transmitted the sum of $12. dollars to Rev. Mr. Buchanan. . .all of which are ordered to be certified to the Convention of this State." (Sgd.) Bryan Fairfax, Minister; W. Payne, C.W., Roger West, C.W.

A Vestry of Fairfax Parish at Alexandria July 16, 1792, takes note of a letter from the Rev. Bryan Fairfax "Communicating. . .his resignation as minister of Fairfax Parish. "Resolved that the Church Wardens wait upon that gentleman and express their concern that the reasons contained in his letter are found to operate to the discontinuance of so meritorious a character as this Minister, and they moreover request him to conclude he has the full approbation of the Vestry for his exemplary conduct and laudable exertions in disseminating the religion he professes. . .and further for his uncommon disinterested conduct in assigning the moneys due him for pew rents, to the Vestry. . .for the purposes of the churches he lately had under his care." Joseph Thomas was appointed Collector of all monies due the parish in and about Alexandria and Andrew Monroe Collector of all money due the Parish at or near The Falls Church. Each was ordered to pay the money to Treasurer Herbert "as fast as he collects it, and be allowed 5 percent commission."

At a meeting on August 16, 1792, the Vestry decided "by a majority vote" not to induct Mr. Bernard Page as Minister, and "Resolved that the Church Wardens write the Rev. Mr. Davis, or any other minister of the Episcopal church whom they think proper, acquainting them that the parish is vacant and desirous of inducting a Minister. Mr. James Wren is discontinued a member of the Vestry at his own request. . .Mr. Nicholas Fitzhugh is appointed. . .in the room of Mr. James Wren." Wren had served continuously since his appointment on November 15, 1766.

THE REVEREND THOMAS DAVIS INDUCTED

"At a Vestry held at The Falls Church for the parish of Fairfax, October 1, 1792, The Church Wardens having reported to the vestry that they had according to Order, written to the Revd. Thomas Davis letting him know that the Parish of Fairfax was vacant and that they were desirous of inducting him as Minister and that the said Davis had accordingly agreed to take upon him the charge of Minister of said Parish and was attending the Vestry in order to be inducted, Resolved by a majority of the Vestry that the Revd. Thomas Davis be now inducted as Minister of the Parish aforesaid and that he hereby is inducted. Resolved that the Church Wardens put him in possession of the glebe as soon as they can conveniently do so, and that they now wait on Mr. Davis and inform him of his Induction. Resolved, as it is agreeable to the Revd. Mr. Thomas Davis, Minister of the Parish, the Vestry grants leave to the Revd. Bernard Page to preach at the two churches in Fairfax Parish on any day that they are not to be occupied by the Minister himself, and that such subscriptions as people chose to make the Revd. Bernard Page the Vestry disclaim any authority in collecting or applying. But the Vestry hereby declare that no pew holder or any renter has any right to appropriate any money they may owe for pew rents to any purpose whatsoever. But they are bound to the Vestry Collector to be appropriated to the use of the Revd. Thomas Davis. W. Payne, C.W., R. West, C.W. "The Reverend Thomas Davis having been inducted into the Parish of Fairfax as Minister. It is agreed between the Minister and Vestry that the Glebe shall be put into his possession by the Church Wardens as soon as he choose to attend to receive it, that the pew rents in the Church at Alexandria and all monies that the Vestry can get subscribed for his use shall be punctually and faithfully collected as is possible for them to have it done. And except the charge of such collections and 30 pounds to be reserved for the use *of the churches,* the money so collected shall annually be paid the Rev. Thomas Davis for his support and services as minister. And the said Mr. Davis hereby engages to live in the parish and officiate and so do the duties of Minister of the Protestant Episcopal Church in the Parish so long, and *to preach at Alexandria and Falls Churches alternately every Sabbath Day when* not prevented therefrom by sickness or bad weather or accident."

During the tenure of the Rev. Thomas Davis as Rector of Fairfax Parish the Vestry computed the valuation of the annual rent of the Glebe to be 30 pounds, and it provided that 15 pounds of this should be paid by him to the Treasurer for the use of The Upper (Falls) Church.

The Vestry elected Easter Monday, 1796, met only three times, according to the records. Bishop William Meade mentions in 1837 that Bishop Madison visited The Falls Church "about 40 years previously," or about 1797. Evidently, The Falls Church was actively in use at that time.

THE VESTRY OF FAIRFAX PARISH FADES AWAY

Two names that had been prominent in Vestry records for many years had disappeared by the time of the April 1797 meeting. William Payne, long a Church Warden, is not listed, nor did he attend that meeting in 1798. The other vestryman with many years of service was Charles Broadwater. He was not in attendance at either the 1797 or 1798 meeting, although he had been a vestryman continuously since 1744. He lived near present-day Vienna and, like Payne, attended The Falls Church.

Since Vestries were elected for three-year periods there should have been an election at Easter 1799. All records are apparently lost for the years 1799 to 1803 inclusive. Sometime in that period the Fairfax Parish Vestry disappeared. Alexandria and Alexandria County (present-day Arlington) came under the District of Columbia in February 1801. The Falls Church remained in Virginia.

A Virginia Act passed in January 1802 permitted any vacant church glebe lands to be sold by the overseers of the poor. The Fairfax Glebe was by that time in the District of Columbia, but it was

1815 before the Supreme Court ruled that it could be sold by the Vestry of the "Episcopal Church in Alexandria."

The next record of a Vestry election and meeting is: "At an election of 12 persons to serve as Vestrymen for 3 years, held on April 2, 1804 at the Protestant Episcopal Church of Alexandria, the following were duly elected: Wm. Herbert, Wm. Fitzhugh, George Taylor, John Roberts, George Deneale, Daniel McLean, Hezekiah Smoot, Richard Conway, James B. Nichols, John Tucker, E.J. Lee and Chas. Sims." Of these Conway, Fitzhugh, Herbert, and Nichols had been members of the Fairfax Vestry whose terms expired at Easter 1799.

The Vestry meetings which follow are all entitled "At a meeting of the Vestry of the Episcopal Church of Alexandria." At a meeting so entitled on September 9, 1806, "The Reverend Thomas Davis, having notified the Vestry that they are not to consider him *Rector* of the *Episcopal* Church of Alexandria after the first of October next, he being about to remove from this place." His resignation was accepted with a suitable resolution of regret.

Mr. Davis had been inducted as Minister of Fairfax Parish at a Vestry held at The Falls Church on October 1, 1792, after signing an agreement to preach alternate Sundays at the Alexandria and The Falls Churches.

From 1799 until 1814 there were no delegates from Virginia at the General Conventions of the Church. Between 1799 and 1812 there is a record of only one Diocesan Convention |1805| . The Protestant Episcopal Church in Virginia was in a deplorable condition. After the Vestry of Fairfax Parish disappeared from existence there was no organized body responsible for The Falls Church. Despite this the Church survived, indicating the presence of a dedicated number of people.

It is noteworthy that the church at Alexandria was consecrated by Bishop Clagett of Maryland as Christ Church in 1813. At that time the petition signed by the Vestry of Christ Church began, "Whereas, as the Vestry of the Parish of Fairfax of Virginia, for the time being, and under the jurisdiction thereof. . ."

The Vestry of Fairfax Parish appears to have engaged in some activity in the year 1823, however, because the lay delegate from The Falls Church, John Moore, endeavored to take his seat at the Diocesan Convention held in Leesburg in May of that year. We learn that the Committee on certification of lay delegates reported that a "certificate purporting to be from the Vestry of Fairfax Parish, held on the 10th day of this month at The Falls Church purporting to appoint John Moore as a lay delegate. . .Having been presented, the

Committee are of the opinion, that if there is an Episcopal Congregation belonging to that church, then it is under the government of the Vestry who have appointed Edmund J. Lee to represent that parish. . ." Mr. Lee was the delegate from Christ Church, Alexandria. Under date of May 14 the minutes read further: "A petition of John Moore was. . .read, setting forth that he was on the 10th instant, duly elected a lay delegate to represent. . .the Congregation of The Falls Church in Fairfax Parish. . .that the Convention refused him a seat, upon the ground that the Parish of Fairfax was properly represented by members of Christ Church in Alexandria within the District of Columbia."

It was the opinion of the Committee on the State of the Church to whom the petition was referred that there was no canon which provides for the division of parishes, nor for more than one representative from a parish. They further contended that in order to have such a division of a parish, it would be necessary to apply to the Convention, submitting a register of the names of those who wish a division. It then would be the decision of the Convention whether such a division should be made.

THE SEMINARY COMES TO THE RESCUE

What happened to The Falls Church congregation after this setback the records do not show. The church was evidently being used for prayer services. The Virginia Theological Seminary was started in Alexandria and moved to Seminary Hill in 1829. The professors and students were engaged in missionary work, as can be seen.

The General Convention in August 1829 received a report on Virginia: "Prospects continue encouraging. Arrangements made for permanent establishment of Theological Seminary in Diocese. Besides the repair of several of our old churches almost in ruins, and the reoccupation of some almost or entirely deserted. . .report the building. . .of several entirely new churches." By 1832 the Diocesan Convention listed "Fairfax Parish, Christ Church, Alexandria, D.C.; St. Paul's, Alexandria, D.C.; The Falls Church, Fairfax County, Va." The canonical change as a result of the Moore petition had borne fruit. Seminarian Launcelot Minor began work at The Falls Church as a lay reader about 1834 and before his graduation in 1836 had a large Sunday School and a congregation.

The Diocesan report for 1836 shows Professor Lippitt of the Seminary as "Minister in Charge." In July 1837 six persons were confirmed by Assistant Bishop Meade, who reported, "Some years since the attention of the professors of our Seminary and some of the students were drawn to it, and occasional services performed. This led to its partial repair."

The Rev. Mr. Lippitt reported to the Diocesan Convention in 1838 that "funds have been raised for the repair of the church which will be put in order it is expected by July. Sunday School and Bible Class are still in flourishing condition." Funerals 1, Baptisms, infants, 3 white, 1 colored. Communicants, Added 2, died 1, total 14. Baptism, 1 infant, funeral 1. The Church has been thoroughly repaired and in interior arrangements remodelled and improved and is now a very convenient and neat place of public worship. . .There will be completed around the church a plain substantial enclosure embracing a burial ground. At the time of the last report the Sunday School was the only one in that neighborhood. Since one has been opened in the Methodist Chapel, about a mile distant, which has diminished very much the attendance. It, however, has 38 scholars. . .10 teachers. . ." Funds for the repairs were provided largely by the generosity of Captain Henry Fairfax, the grandson of the Reverend Bryan Fairfax.

THE REVEREND R.T. BROWN, MINISTER AT THE FALLS CHURCH

During the next twenty years (1840-1860) the church seems to have achieved a stable situation. Captain Henry Fairfax's name appears as lay delegate from The Falls Church to the Diocesan Convention in 1840 and 1841. The Rev. Richard Templeton Brown became minister in October 1842 following Professor Lippit's departure from the Seminary. The following spring, May 1843, Henry Denison was named lay delegate to the Diocesan Convention from The Falls Church.

Concerning his new charge, the Rev. Mr. Brown reported, "I took charge of this venerable church in October last. . .found but 10 communicants and 6 families. . .Since. . .the following changes . . .Communicants, died 1, added 10, total 20. Baptisms, adult 2, infant 2, total 4. Funerals 3. Families in constant attendance. . .16. A Bible Class and Sabbath School and services for. . .the colored are also established at the church under care of brethren from the Theological Seminary," and he adds, "The whole country receives constantly large accessions to its population from the northern states."

A number of services when Bishop William Meade and Assistant Bishop John Johns were present were held in the years between 1843 and 1846. Mr. Brown left the parish in 1844 and The Falls Church was without a minister. The Seminary "brethren" once again kept things going because Bishop Meade reported that he confirmed one person at the Little Falls Church in June 1845. James A. Woodward, a senior seminarian, represented The Falls Church at the Diocesan Convention in 1846. During that same year Alexandria and Alexandria

County were retroceded to Virginia, and in September Bishop Johns preached at The Falls Church.

An important footnote to this period is the death of Captain Henry Fairfax at Saltillo, Mexico, on August 14, 1846. His remains were brought home for burial in the churchyard, at his own request. He was 41 years old. It was Captain Fairfax who financed the restoration of The Falls Church in the 1830's and 1840's. He was a graduate of West Point, who organized a company called the Fairfax Volunteers at the outbreak of the Mexican War.

THE REVEREND WM. P. LOCKWOOD AS MINISTER

In May 1846, the Convention reports show Rev. Wm. P. Lockwood as Minister of The Falls Church and of Zion at Fairfax. He resigned in October 1852, but earlier that year he stated, "Dr. May and Dr. Packard had supplied Falls Church twice a month to enable me to have services at St. John's, Centerville. (This latter church had been organized through his efforts and had been consecrated when it became free of debt by Bishop Meade in July 1851.) In May 1853, the Diocesan Report showed 17 communicants. It further added, "Since November Professors May and Packard have supplied the pulpit every alternate Sunday. Mr. Claxton, a student at the Seminary, who superintends the Sunday School, reads the service on those Sundays when there is no preaching, so that the church is open...every Sunday. This arrangement will continue until a Rector is called..." The records show that Arthur Lee Bryant was a lay delegate to the Diocesan Conventions of 1850 and 1851 from The Falls Church. Mr. Claxton was lay delegate in 1854.

Early in 1855, Rev. R.T. Brown returned to serve The Falls Church in Fairfax Parish and Zion and St. John's in Truro Parish. Apparently, he lived in Falls Church until 1858 and at Fairfax Court House in 1859 and 1860. In 1858 Bishop Meade was living at Millwood and Assistant Bishop Johns, near the Seminary. While the number of communicants at The Falls Church was not large, it remained constant as the 1856 Diocesan Report shows 20 communicants, 18 families, 3 baptisms and 3 funerals. The May 1860 report shows 7 baptisms, 1 funeral and 22 communicants.

VIRGINIA INVADED

Once again the dogs of war were casting their shadows across the land. Both Bishop Johns and Mr. Brown attended the Diocesan Convention at St. Paul's, Richmond, on May 16, 1861. The former recounts his impressions: "On Friday morning, May 24, at an early hour the Federal forces took possession of Alexandria. It was now evident that I could no longer remain there unless I was prepared to be separated from the Diocese and restricted in official duties. . . In two hours after the invasion I was on the road with those of my family who had not previously moved."

The Rev. Mr. Brown and his family were living at Fairfax in the house which is now the rectory of Truro Church. The diary of Mrs. McGuire, wife of the Rev. Mr. McGuire, Principal of Episcopal High School, states: "Fairfax, C.H., May 25, 1861. Alexandria and environs, including, I greatly fear, our home is in the hands of the enemy. . .About sunset (yesterday) we drove up to the door of this, the house of our relatives, the Rev. Mr. Brown. . ." A later entry says, "Chantilly, June 1. We came here this morning. About 3 in the night we were aroused by a volley of musketry not far from our windows. . .We soon saw a body of cavalry moving up the street. . .They passed below our windows. . .another volley, and to my unpracticed ears. . .a discharge of a thousand muskets. . .the cavalry strained by. . .we witnessed the retreat of 85 of the 2nd U.S. Cavalry. They had been sent out from Arlington we suppose to reconnoiter. . .we observed. . .placing sentinels on Mr. Brown's porch. . .another raid was expected. The gentlemen ordered the carriages and in half an hour Mr. Brown's family and ourselves were on our way to this place."

History shows that Virginia voted to secede from the Union on May 23. That same day, Federal forces had occupied Arlington Heights and the bridges across the Potomac to protect the Capital. On the following day, May 24, the Confederate Congress approved moving its Capital to Richmond. Confederate troops soon assembled about Manassas Junction, and the village of Falls Church was caught between the opposing armies.

WAR COMES TO THE FALLS CHURCH

By 1861 a small village had grown up about The Falls Church, and three other churches had come to the community. The Methodist Chapel was on the present Oakwood Cemetery site, the Baptist Church on the Broad Street lot now owned by The Falls Church, and the Presbyterians were meeting in a community building near their present Church. The Alexandria, Loudoun and Hampshire Railroad had been completed to Leesburg a few years previously. The influx of people from the north reported by the Reverend Mr. Brown in 1843 had continued, and the people were of divided opinion on the war issues. Even families were divided.

Frank Leslies' Illustrated, in the issue of June 29, 1861, "Falls

Church; This is a Village in Virginia. . .our artist has sent us an interesting sketch (made June 19) of the arrival of Lieutenant Tompkins and his gallant Co. B. at that Village. . .Lieutenant Tompkins has already distinguished himself by the dashing charge at Fairfax Court House. . ." This charge was described not quite this way by Mr. McGuire as noted above. Company B was now part of the advance to Bull Run. After the battle there on July 21 the Federal Army streamed back towards Washington. The Confederates followed and occupied Fairfax Court House.

UNION FORCES MAKE A STAND AT FALLS CHURCH

On August 3, 1861, a correspondent for *Harper's Weekly* writes: "On this page we illustrate Falls Church, Fairfax County, Va., from a sketch by our special artist with General McDowell's Corps d' Armee. This is the most advanced post of our army. . .and has been the scene of several picket skirmishes. Falls Church was built in 1709 and rebuilt, as an inscription on the wall informs us, by the late Lord Fairfax, whose son the present Lord Fairfax, is supposed to be serving with the rebel army. The inscription on the old church reads as follows: 'Henry Fairfax, an accomplished gentleman, an upright magistrate, a sincere Christian, died in command of the Fairfax Volunteers at Saltillo, Mexico, 1847. But for his munificence this church might still have been a ruin.' " The same article states, "Service was held in the old church two Sundays since, Rev. Dr. Sims, Chaplain of the Second Maine Regiment officiating, and most of the troops of the neighborhood being present."

THE CONFEDERATES OCCUPY FALLS CHURCH

On August 28, 1861, Col. J.E.B. Stuart, then on Munson's Hill, reports to General Longstreet, "The 1st Regiment is at Falls Church, and I have directed its commander to hold himself in readiness. . ." On September 25, General Joseph E. Johnston reports to Richmond, ". . .eleven regiments of infantry and Col. Stuart's Cavalry stationed at Falls Church, Munson's and Mason's Hills, at Padgett's and Springfield Station."

Some days later, the Confederates withdrew from Falls Church to Fairfax. An article in *Leslies'* of October 26, 1861, states, "By the recent withdrawal of the Rebel forces Falls Church has again come into our possession and is the headquarters of General Smith." On November 18, a skirmish was reported between Lt. Colonel Fitz Lee, 1st Va. Cavalry, and Lt. Col. Fowler, about a mile south of Falls Church. On November 20, President Lincoln inspected a "Grand Review" of McClellan's Army at Bailey's Crossroads. That fall, Fort Buffalo was constructed near Seven Corners by the 21st N.Y. Infantry (recruited at Buffalo, N.Y.). The Federal forces remained in control of the village and of the church for the remainder of the war. There were skirmishes and raids, but the only serious threat was in 1862 after the second battle at Bull Run. Mosby's Rangers raided the area at times and were a threat to Union forces until 1865.

THE CHURCH AS A BRIGADE HOSPITAL

The church was first occupied as a hospital by the Army in 1861, according to official reports, and was later used as a stable, etc., by various bodies of troops in the neighborhood. Mr. Charles A. Stewart in his manuscript, "The Falls Church," states, "Mr. Benjamin Shreve (1936). . .recalls a visit to the church when it was occupied. . .as a hospital. He was. . .fourteen, and had been sent with his sister to take some refreshments to a wounded Confederate prisoner. . .the officer in charge was very courteous and escorted him and his young sister to the soldier lying ill in one of the pews. The captured Confederate was given the same care as other wounded. . .there must have been . . .a hundred wounded soldiers inside the church, two or three in each box-like pew. . ." Mr. W.N. Lynch (1940). . .has a vivid recollection of much that occurred around the old church. . .Born in 1855, he was a boy of ten when the war ended. His uncle, the late John Lynch, was sexton of the church for many years. Mr. Lynch in referring to the. . .interior of the church before its desecration by Federal troops said the middle aisle was paved with tile, and he remembers the high backed pews. He also recalled the Apostles' Creed painted on the wall to the left of the altar. The main entrance then was the south door, and the high pulpit with steps leading up to it faced this door. There were more trees in the churchyard then than now. A number of Confederate soldiers killed in skirmishes not far away were buried in the churchyard. Two were buried in front of the west entrance; the remains of one, he said, were later exhumed and buried elsewhere. Mr. Lynch as a lad was well acquainted with Bishop Southgate, the first rector. . .after the war, and often visited his home, now known as the Wilson Place, just across Fairfax St. from the church. Mr. Lynch said that the church, when appropriated by the army, was first used by soldiers of the 14th N.Y. Cavalry as a hospital, and that later the floor was torn out and the building turned into a stable."

THE CHURCH SAVED FROM DESTRUCTION

Mr. Charles A. Stewart in his *Virginia Village* states, "The damage done to the Church, according to Mr. George B. Ives, was done by a company of Union Cavalry on picket duty under command of a captain of the regular army. He permitted his men to tear out the floor of the church and use it as a stable. The building might have been damaged beyond repair, had it not been for Mr. Ives and the late John Bartlett, who reported the matter to General Augur, the military governor of the district, by whose orders the captain was arrested."

The plate honoring Henry Fairfax disappeared from the front wall of the church, and the inscription on his monument in the churchyard was taken from the *Harper's Weekly* quotation given above. The plates with the Commandments and the Creed furnished by James Wren were carried away, according to a report, to a church in Hartford, Connecticut. A silver communion chalice was taken by an officer in a New York Regiment, and it was returned to the church by his granddaughter in 1952. There is a story passed down by word of mouth that a soldier boxed up the stone baptismal font and left it at the Star Tavern in Falls Church. The tavern keeper returned it to some church people, who kept it until the church was opened again. Eleven of the original tiles laid in the aisles torn up by Union soldiers were collected in the neighborhood by Mrs. W.L. Ribble, wife of the Rector from 1935 to 1945.

The Brady photographs of 1861 show the church exterior as unchanged from 1768. The lower windows each have 18 panes, there are stone steps at the doors, the pediment at the west door is undamaged and there is a brick and stone pediment *at the south door.* In a later photograph of about 1900, the Army repairs are visible in the patched pediment at the west door. The lower windows each have 12 panes, the pediment of the south door is of wood, and the patched places under the lower windows in the west wall and under the two lower westerly windows of the south wall are clearly shown.

Bishop Meade died on March 14, 1862, and Assistant Bishop John Johns succeeded him. In May 1862, the annual assembly of clergy and laity of Virginia, until then known as "Convention," was changed to "Council." The Virginia Church in 1861 had helped organize the Council of the Church in the Confederate States. The State Council met each year during the war. Bishop Johns reported to the May 1862 council that the Reverend R.T. Brown had taken letters dismissary to South Carolina.

THE ARMY REPAIRS THE CHURCH

The Bishop in his report to the Council meeting at St. Paul's, Alexandria, on May 16, 1866, said: "On March 11, I preached in The

Falls Church, Fairfax County. This venerable building, which had been so appropriately fitted up before the War, was so damaged by military use, and the congregation so dispersed that all hope of renewing services there, at least for some years, was abandoned. In February last an officer connected with the Quarter Master Department called at my residence to say that he had superintended the expenditure of an appropriation by the Government for repairing the church, which was now in a condition to be occupied, and to request that some arrangement be made to open it statedly for religious services. This was promptly done by the professors and students of the Seminary. Though the building has lost much of its former church-like appearance, it has been judiciously repaired, according to the means appropriated, and the people of the Parish are again in possession of a comfortable house of worship, for which they are indebted to the disinterested and preserving zeal of Mr. Jacob C. DePutron, of whose efficient good will I take pleasure in making this honorable record." Mr. Stewart in "The Falls Church" states: Mr. DePutron "entered the war in May 1861 in Co. E., 71st Pa. Infantry, fought in many battles. . .and was mustered out in July 1864. . .married a Falls Church lady, Miss Mary Elizabeth Sherwood, April 26, 1866. . .made his home in this town and engaged in the practise of law. . .He died in Falls Church in 1926 and was buried in Arlington Cemetery." Mr. DePutron was a member of the first Vestry organized after the war in 1873.

Also in "The Falls Church" is a letter of February 23, 1936, from the late A. L. Anderson, then a Civil Engineer in the Quarter Master General's office, reporting on the repairs made to the church by the Army after the war. Mr. Anderson was a member of the Falls Church. "The records . . . show the receipt on November 20, 1865 of a claim for the restoration of The Falls Church building . . . damaged . . . during the War . . . and that on December 20, 1865 Col. M. J. Ludington . . . was directed . . . to restore the Church at Falls Church . . . so as to be fit for worship. The total expense not to exceed $1300. The records fail to show how this work was done, whether by contract or by the labor of a hired carpenter . . . The report of the Chief Quarter Master, Department of Washington, December 14, 1865, shows that the church building was first occupied in the summer of 1861 . . . for use as a hospital and was subsequently occupied by various bodies of troops from time to time as a stable, etc., until the summer of 1865. No rent was allowed, or paid, for the use of the building."

At the time of the last restoration, the wainscoting on the south doorway returns, the writings on the plaster could be plainly read:

On East Side	On West Side	
Thos. Walsh	A. W. Carpenter	D. C. Davis
A. H. Barnes	F. Allen	Co. G.
Mch. 6, 1865	Co. B. 13 N.Y. Inf.	21st N.Y. Cavalry
Mass	July 1 - 1861	

Under the wainscoting on the south wall, east of the most westerly window the following appeared:

Lorin Clifford
3rd Mass. Cavalry - Co. J.
May 21 -

These writings date the wainscoting at sometime after 1865. Those in the doorway returns could have been before or after the church was gutted. The name "Clifford" must have been written after the pew woodwork against the wall was torn off. It is apparent that the original construction did not include woodwork in these doorway returns, and the writings there show that no plaster repairs were made there after the War.

From the evidence largely visible, the work done by the Army included the brick repairs noted, 12 new lower windows and new frames for six of them, new doors at the west and south entrances, new timber frame work at the south doorway and some new shingles and minor roof repairs. It also included new plastering in places on the north and east walls where the woodwork of the Wren altar piece and pulpit and canopy had been torn out, an entire new floor, a wainscoting on all four walls up to the lower line of the window openings, a platform in the east, used until the 1906 remodelling, and whitewashing the walls and ceiling. In addition, a number of bench type pews were added. The price of $1300 would have been sufficient in 1865 to do that work with the low prices for labor and materials prevailing in a countryside laid waste by war.

Already venerable at the close of the War Between the States, the historic Falls Church had been a recruiting station during the Revolutionary War. In *Virginia's Colonial Churches*, Mr. Rawlings points out that it had been used earlier by a regiment of Braddock's Army in the French and Indian War. In the War of 1812 the British are said to have searched the church for our fleeing President. The greatest damage, however, was done by the Federal troops during the war years of 1861-1865.[4] The ebb and flow of American history had left its tidewater mark for all time on The Falls Church.

---

[4] James Scott Rawlings, *Virginia's Colonial Churches* (Richmond, Va.: Garrett and Massie, 1963), p. 217.

Fig. 1. *The West Door. (Brady 1862) The man seated is reputed to be Matthew Brady. The paling fence was built in 1839.*

Fig. 2. *The South Side of The Falls Church (Matthew Brady) Note the South Door and the paling fence in foreground.*

Fig. 3. *Enlargement of South Door and stone steps shown in Fig. 5.*

Fig. 4. *Federal Cavalry at The Falls Church (a later Matthew Brady photograph, probably 1863.) The paling fence has been removed.*

Fig. 5. *The South Side (Matthew Brady). The paling fence has been removed. Note the original stone doorway and stone steps.*

Fig. 6. *Columbia Baptist Church by Matthew Brady. The east side of The Falls Church is visible in background.*

Fig. 7. *An interior view of the East Wall (Matthew Brady) showing the Ten Commandments and The Apostles' Creed. One tablet has been removed. The upper center window is covered on the inside.*

Fig. 8. *North Wall during 1959 restoration showing original ceiling rafters and curved pieces for cornice and the nailing strip inset in the wall to which 1768 canopy was nailed. (Photo by Charles E. Gage, 1959)*

Fig. 9. *Exterior corner showing Flemish bond below water table in 1768 masonry. (Lee Briggs, 1969)*

Fig. 10. *Corner 1768 masonry, showing rounded brick in water table. (Lee Briggs, 1969)*

Fig. 11. *West Doorway. . .*
Upper part shows
original orange
brick of 1768.
Lower part shows
patch work in red
brick of 1866.
Compare with same
doorway in Fig. 1.
(Lee Briggs, 1969)

Fig. 12. *South and West sides of The Falls Church about 1906. (Approx-*
imate appearance between 1866 and 1906)

Fig. 13. *Interior in 1908 with the oil lamps and pews of 1866 still in use.*

Fig. 14. *The South and West sides in 1947. (Porter Studios)*

Fig. 15. *The Baptismal Font, which survived since colonial days. (Lee Briggs)*

Fig. 16. *8 February 1958—Interior of old church as it appeared before rebuilding and renewal of 1959. Note the organ speakers above the panels in each corner. Organ console in right corner.*

Fig. 17. *At the Service of Rededication in January 1960, reading from l. to r.: Rev. W. Leigh Ribble, Rev. Wallace Shields, Rt. Rev. Frederick D. Goodwin, Rev. J. Hodge Alves, and Rev. Francis W. Hayes, Jr. This photograph was taken on the north side at the cloister rail. (H. Hunter)*

Fig. 18. *The interior of The Falls Church following the extensive redecoration of 1959. (Lee Briggs)*

Fig. 19. *The North and West sides in 1969, showing the cloister leading from the church to the parish house. (Lee Briggs)*

Fig. 20. *The 1769 church and the 1952 Parish Hall. (Lee Briggs)*

Fig. 21. *The architect's rendering of the 1769 church, the 1952 addition and the 1959 addition.*

Fig. 22. *The completed church structure (1960)*

Fig. 23. *Another view of the church (1960)*

Fig. 24. *Holy Table and Palladian window (1960)*

pARt II

life flows Back into
the falls chuRch:
1865
to the
thiRò RestoRation

With the end of the war, the return of some normalcy to the community and the crude, but adequate restoration done by the United States Army, the venerable building of The Falls Church became once again a house of worship.

In 1862 at the Council of the Diocese of Virginia, with the Rt. Rev. John Johns, D.D., presiding, the Committee on the State of the Church said in its report (of which Mr. Stewart says, "No doubt this refers to The Falls Church"): "Church after church has been shut up, and in some cases abused and desecrated; minister after minister has been compelled to leave his house and charge, sometimes to flee for his life, congregation after congregation has been broken up and dispersed.—The very worst case of flagrant outrage in this respect, occurred within ten miles of Washington."

Four years later in May 1866, at St. Paul's, Alexandria, Bishop Johns in his Council address, speaking of The Falls Church, said that not many months past the building was so badly damaged and the congregation so dispersed he had abandoned hope for any early resumption of services. But, he continued, the activity of staunch friends had induced the government to repair, at least in part, the damage caused by the soldiers. He had already opened The Falls Church for divine services and had preached there on March 11, and faculty and students of the Episcopal Theological Seminary had consented to hold stated religious services at The Falls Church. There has always been, then as now, a close and fruitful relationship between the Seminary and this congregation.

Worship services were now held regularly in the old church by the men from the Seminary, though there was no formal organization of the congregation until 1873. Records of these eight years are few. We know, however, that Bishop Johns gave permission to the Methodists to hold some services in The Falls Church. Melvin Lee Steadman in *Falls Church, By Fence and Fireside,* in speaking about the Methodists says, "Early in 1866 arrangements were made with the Episcopalians to hold services in old Falls Church. The Southerns' group appointed a committee to call on Bishop Johns of the Episcopal Seminary to arrange for the use of the church. The desired permission was obtained, but Bishop Johns made the remark 'that the Methodists should erect a building as soon as possible, as two old ladies cannot agree for very long in the same house.' Dr. Joseph Packard of the Seminary preached to the Methodist group from time to time."

This ecumenical story illustrates that there existed many years ago the spirit of cooperation between the churches in Falls Church, which seems to have prevailed through much of its history. It is probable that Dr. Packard's preaching to the Methodists was during his "stated services," when the Methodists joined in a union service with whatever congregation might have been gathered together. There was in those days in many places a custom that certain Sundays were known as "Methodist Sunday" or "Episcopal Sunday." However, the Methodists did not continue for long to use the building. On May 30, 1869 Dulin Methodist Church was consecrated.

Another interesting story of this period is told by Mr. Stewart. It seems that some of the members of the old Falls Church, freshly returned from war, lacked reverence and polished manners. A young ex-soldier noted for a positive manner and a ready use of expletives became a layreader. One day, as he was reading the service, several young men standing just outside the front door, continued loud and boisterous conversation, which was disturbing the congregation. The young layreader stopped the service, left the chancel and strode to the door. Shaking his fist at the noisy young men, he exclaimed, "How in the hell can I read the service, when you fellows are making such a noise out here at the door? Please come quietly in and worship with us." Whether they became worshippers or not, we are not told, but Mr. Stewart adds, "It is needless to say the disturbance did not occur again."

PERMANENT ORGANIZATION COMES IN 1873

1873 saw the dawn of a new era for The Falls Church. Of this Mr. Stewart writes, "Since that time the congregation has been going in and out of its doors regularly. For more than sixty-seven years its ministers have exercised a beneficent influence among its own members as well as in the community at large."

The congregation of The Falls Church was formally reorganized November 27, 1873. For eight years the Journal of the Diocese had shown no report from this congregation, but now this dreary record would cease. After due notice, all who were interested in the establishment of a permanent congregation and the election of a Vestry according to the canons of the Diocese of Virginia met in the old church. Mr. George E. Porter was called to the chair and Mr. J.C. DePutron was elected "acting Secretary." Those elected to the Vestry were:

George E. Porter, Senior Warden	George C. Ely
Sackett Duryee, Junior Warden	H.J. England
N.F. Graham, Treasurer	Levi Parker
J.C. DePutron, Secretary	

Most of these men were Northerners, many of them soldiers who had come to know the Falls Church area first during the war. They had returned to work in the government or because they had come to love the countryside. They came quickly to worship and work with the former members who had remained or returned; and, few as they were, they set about quickly to build up the church. The Vestry met within two weeks to undertake needed repairs to the old building and to make plans to collect funds for this purpose. A list of needs was drawn up, including paint for interior $20, window shades $40 and lamps $30. It was also decided to repair the chimney as soon as money could be raised. At the next meeting in December, De-Putron reported lamps purchased for $52.75 and the Vestry authorized immediate repairs to the chimney. There was no report on the raising of money, but it must have had some success.

Alas, however, there were difficulties in those days and a tendency to "weary in well doing." The Annual meeting of the congregation was held April 6, 1874, and there seem to have been few in attendance; for each of the first four vestrymen elected received only 5 votes and Mr. George G. Ely received 4 votes. The Vestrymen elected were:

George E. Porter	J.C. DePutron
Sackett Duryee	George G. Ely
N.F. Graham	

BISHOP SOUTHGATE BECOMES THE FIRST POST-WAR RECTOR

Living in the village of Falls Church at this time was the Rt. Rev. Horatio Southgate, D.D., formerly Missionary Bishop of Constantinople and Rector of churches in Boston and New York. Immediately after its election in April 1874 the Vestry called Bishop Southgate to be the first post-war Rector at a salary of $100 per annum plus offerings to be taken at the services and special offerings to be taken occasionally. It was a blessing to the struggling congregation that the Bishop not only agreed to accept the call to lead in the rebuilding of this disrupted body, but declined to accept any remuneration, except the offerings made at regular services held by him and his official expenses which would be approximately $100 a year.

Bishop Southgate had a strong personality and continued to be remembered for many years. His home, across Fairfax Street from the church, was known by his name long after he had left it. During his ministry the congregation grew larger and stronger and much was done to improve the building and grounds of the old church. "Heating apparatus" was bought when the chimney was repaired. The churchyard fence was completed with two wrought iron gates on the West Front, "one larger for vehicles and one small for persons." A regular sexton was employed at $12 per annum. The Bishop served The Falls Church for more than two years, but continued to live in the village much longer. He died in Astoria, N.Y., in 1894.

THE VESTRY OATH OF THE DIOCESE OF VIRGINIA

Thrilling moments come to one who peruses Vestry minutes of a century ago. Suddenly, I turned to a page in beautiful Spencarian writing. It was a record of the Vestrymen taking the same oath as is still taken by our Vestry members today:

DECLARATION AND PROMISE
of Vestrymen
Diocese of Virginia

"*I do believe* the Holy Scriptures of the Old and New Testament to be the Word of God, and to contain all things necessary to salvation; and I do give my hearty assent and approbation to the doctrines, worship and discipline of the Protestant Episcopal Church in this United States; and I promise that I will faithfully execute the office of Vestryman of Falls Church, in Fairfax County according to my best knowledge and skill."

Cassius F. Lee	Lyman Ballard
Silas D. Tripp	E.W. Watkins
L.E. Gott	Geo. D. Nicolson
L.M. Blackford	W.E. Parker
L. Parker	Geo. E. King
John H. Chichester	S.L. Terrett
Geo. G. Ely	Henry E. Alvord
J.M. Mason	Chas A. Stewart
James B. Hodgkin	

Here were signatures of good and famous men who had carried the ministry of The Falls Church through many years. Many were known to members now living.

Immediately following this page is a brief record of a "Meeting of the congregation of Falls Church, Va., held in the church in pursuance of the canon for the election of a Vestry to hold office for the year ending Easter Monday, 1877." At the request of the Senior Warden, Mr. Porter, the Rev. Thomas Spencer (soon to become "First Professor of the new Bishop Payne Divinity School" as told in the history of that school) called the meeting to order with prayer and acted as chairman. "On motion of Mr. Spencer, seconded by the Senior Warden, the number of the Vestry was extended to seven." The election of the Vestry added to that body several prominent laymen of the county. Cassius F. Lee, Treasurer and Trustee of Virginia Seminary, was elected Junior Warden. Launcelot Minor Blackford, Principal of Episcopal High School 1870-1913, was elected Treasurer. (The author's grandfather, Samuel Johnston Alves, came from Kentucky around 1870 to study under Dr. Blackford.) Mr. Silas D. Tripp came on the Vestry to begin a long and devoted relationship. A tablet on the south wall of the church memorializes his forty years of service.

This Vestry at its first meeting April 30 set up a rather ambitious program. It was decided to seek funds for a new roof and other repairs needed in the church. Cassius Lee agreed to raise funds for these purposes. He and Mr. Blackford agreed to pay half of the cost of ceiling the church. It was also agreed to purchase a suitable organ. Mr. and Mrs. J.E. Engle agreed to attend to the finding of a proper organ.

When Bishop Southgate ceased to have charge we do not know, but the presence and actions of the Rev. Thomas Spencer lead one to believe he was acting as the minister, although he was never formally called. During this time Mr. P.P. Phillips, Seminarian, was listed as layreader.

Occasionally during this period the Vestry met at the Episcopal High School, often without a minister. The new roof of juniper cypress shingles on the church was completed by Smoot and Perry of Alexandria. Finally, the Ladies' Gleaner Society stepped in to help "clean up the debt." "The thanks of the Vestry were, on motion, returned to the minister, the Rev. D.L. Riddle and to the session of the Presbyterian Church for the use of their house of worship, on the Sundays during the repairs on our own. The Register is requested to communicate appropriately the same. L.M. Blackford, Register *pro tem.*" On February 8, 1877, we have the first action to arrange for Trustees: "*Resolved* that application be made to the Court of Fairfax County, for the appointment of Cassius F. Lee, L.M. Blackford and Silas D. Tripp as trustees to hold real estate (Church building land) belonging to Falls Church, Fairfax County, as provided by the statute."

The Falls Church also began to take its place in the Diocese. On April 9, immediately after the election and organization of the Vestry, "Mr. Cassius F. Lee was elected delegate to represent the church in the Diocesan Council to be held in Staunton on Wednesday, the 18th day of May next."

THE REV. JOHN MCGILL SERVES FOUR TIMES

At a meeting of the Vestry, Aug. 19, 1877, Mr. Blackford, Chairman of the committee appointed to confer with the Rev. John McGill, reported that Mr. McGill was ready "to accede to the wish of the Vestry and become the Rector as soon as the proposed salary of $200 could be offered." After much discussion the members of the Vestry increased their pledges toward the first year salary of a rector until $206 was promised. "The Register was then unanimously instructed to extend to the Rev. John McGill of Fairfax County a call to the rectorship of Falls Church and to guaranty to him a salary of $200—payable quarterly in advance; the understanding being that Mr. McGill officiates reguarly at the church two Sunday afternoons in the month." The letters exchanged by Mr. Blackford and the Rev. Mr. McGill are interesting:

Aug. 20, 1877

Rev. & Dear Sir:

As Register of the Vestry of Falls Church, Fairfax County, I am authorized to write to you to take charge of that church as its Rector, giving it two afternoon services each month, at a salary of Two Hundred ($200) dollars per annum, payable quarterly in advance. This compensation is guarantied by the Vestry. It is our desire that your engagement with us should begin September 1st.

Be kind enough to inform me at your earliest convenience of your acceptance of our invitation, and be good enough further to state what day you will hold your first services at Falls Church.

The hour hitherto customary is 4 P.M., at least during the summer.

I am, dear Sir, very faithfully your friend, and Servant in the Church.

/S   L.M. Blackford, Register

Chantilly P.O., Va.
Aug. 22nd, 1877

My Dear Sir:

The call to take charge of The Falls Church extended me by the Vestry of that Church, through you reached me yesterday.

I Accept the call as stated in your letter, and (D.V.) will enter upon my duties, as desired by the Vestry in Sept. and will hold my first service on the second Sunday at the usual hours as stated by you, viz: 4 p.m.

May our united prayers ascend for God's blessing upon the relation which is to subsist between us.

Most sincerely,
(sgd) Jno. McGill

Mr. McGill was a member of the Virginia Seminary Class of 1861, which graduated into the War. He served as Chaplain of the 52nd Virginia Infantry. Although he stayed only eight months, his coming was the beginning of a long and devoted relationship. He was to return three times to minister to the congregation, and his deep affection is shown in his willingness to serve even when he was a sick man. The love borne for Dr. McGill, as he soon became, by members of The Falls Church is a unique and beautiful part of this history.

On April 8, 1878, Mr. McGill told the Vestry that he had received a call to St. Paul's and Emmanuel Churches, Culpeper. He had at first declined, but the call was now repeated, and because of his health he felt he should accept it. The work at Fairfax Court House and Falls Church was much more demanding than at Culpeper. The Vestry offered to raise $125. a year to employ an assistant to be chosen by the Rector. It also approached the Vestry at Fairfax Court House asking that they do the same. To this they agreed.

Two weeks later the Rector wrote from his home in Chantilly stating that with deep appreciation and regret he found it best to accept the call to Culpeper. Therefore, he wrote, "Because I find the work in my present charge to be beyond my strength I hereby tender you my resignation.—Although I have been laboring less than a year among you. I have learned to love you and I grieve at being forced to part from you.—I commend you to the care of our Covenant—Keeping God—May you at last be presented before Him without spot or wrinkle through the atoning merit of the blood of the Lamb of God. Yours affectionately, John McGill."

The vestry in accepting this resignation expressed for themselves and the congregation and "Christian people generally about. our grief at parting from Mr. McGill; and bore witness to the remarkable efficiency of his ministrations among us." On leaving Mr. McGill reported a list of 22 communicants.

THE REV. FRANK PAGE—1878-79

The Rev. Frank Page. Deacon. brother of the famous author. Thomas Nelson Page and of the Hon. Rosewell Page. immediately on graduation from Virginia Seminary in 1878. was appointed by Bishop Whittle to be in charge of Falls Church and Zion Church. Fairfax Courthouse. (There was little concern in those days for ecclesiastical titles. for the minutes begin immediately to call Mr. Page "The Rector." even though he was only a deacon.)

The Rev. Samuel A. Wallis. in his chapter "Seminary Mission Stations." written for the Centennial "History of The Theological Seminary in Virginia" |1923| says "The Falls Church was for some years connected with the Seminary until it was united with Zion Church. Fairfax Courthouse. under the Rev. John McGill and Frank Page."

Frank Page soon became "Rector" of The Falls Church in fact and served the congregation for eleven years. The Rev. Frank Hayes. in an address on the 225th Anniversary of the founding of The Falls Church. said. "Mr. Page's eleven years were not all rosy. as the Vestry minutes report with monotonous regularity that his salary was in arrears and that several members refused to serve on the Vestry when elected. At one point the Rector submitted his resignation on account of illness. There must also have been other reasons. as the arrearage in his salary was increasing. he had little income and the Vestry had reduced the amount of the salary without his consent." The Vestry refused to accept his resignation and gave him a two-months leave. Mr. Page consented to continue.

The Vestry minutes of this period are brief and we do not have many other resources. There was a growing concern about the cemetery. especially. "the number of unauthorized interments." In 1879 the Vestry "resolved that. owing to the room there being almost exhausted, no interment should be allowed in the graveyard of the Church except of persons of the Episcopal Church who have already members of the family interred there." A most interesting letter was written to the Town Council:

> To the Honorable Council
> of the Town of Falls Church
> Gentlemen:
> The undersigned, a committee of the Vestry of the Episcopal Church in this town appointed for the purpose, beg leave respectfully to submit for your consideration the following statement.
> The yard of this Church is the only place for burials in or near the town, so that it is now rapidly filling by interments of persons in no way connected with the congregation to which it belongs, and who are laid there less from the preference of their friends than from the necessity of the case. We are naturally anxious that this should not continue, and think it not inappropriate that some measures looking to our relief should be taken by your body.
> The present size and importance of the town demand a public cemetery, and we respectfully suggest that efforts toward providing one be at once inaugurated. It cannot surely be the desire of the Council, or those whom they represent, that a burial place belonging to a single congregation should continue the only one for the entire community, and it seems neither just nor expedient that such should be the case.
> We are, gentlemen, with much respect,
> Very truly yours, Levi Parker,
> S.E. Gott, L.M. Blackford

The Council then voted to create a public cemetery.

July 6, 1879 a special meeting was called evidently to consider allowing the Rector a vacation. The only action was "unanimously agreed the Rector, the Rev. Frank Page, be invited to take, at such time during the present year (1879) as he may prefer; a vacation of one month; the Register to signify the same to Mr. Page."

On April 20, 1880, the Register reported to the Vestry that Mrs. George Ely, who had long been collecting silver from members and others for a Communion service, had recently presented the completed service to the Rector. A unanimous vote of thanks was extended to Mrs. Ely. This Communion service was regularly loaned to Episcopal High School for many years and is one of the sets still used regularly at The Falls Church. (1967).

The outstanding occurrence of Mr. Page's years was the presentation of a layreader of the congregation, Mr. Jabez Koon, as a candidate for Holy Orders. He was one of the first to be recorded of only six or eight presented through the whole history of The Falls Church. In a letter to Mr. Charles Stewart written by Mr. Page in 1915, he said,

"Sometime I will tell you about getting Mr. Jabez Koon—a Sunday School Teacher and Layreader at The Falls Church—to go into the ministry. He died only a few years ago. Lee Kinsolving, now Bishop of Brazil, was confirmed in The Falls Church, when he was a boy at the High School about '79 or '80. Dr. L.M. Blackford and Mr. Cassius Lee helped to keep the church going, as vestrymen. When I resigned and went to Texas in 1889, funds were short. Dr. Blackford eventually paid me the back salary.

Like you, I think Captain Fairfax and George Somerville were powerful factors in old Falls Church, as I think Dr. Blackford and Mr. Lee were then. Dr. Gott was a vestryman a long time. In 1878 Mr. Tripp was a vestryman and the Parkers were communicants when it seemed we were dragging bottom. I will show you my papers sometime.

Cordially yrs,
Frank Page

Things seemed to go better in the last years of Mr. Page's ministry, except for the continual and rather large balance due on his salary. For the first time "the envelope system of offerings" was introduced. Yet at the end of his tenth year he gave "an informal address" to the Vestry "expressing satisfaction at the general condition of things in the congregation." Finally on Nov. 19, 1889, Mr. Page submitted his letter of resignation to the Vestry "to accept a call to Waco, Texas." He ended, "I ask you to forgive any shortcomings of my Rectorship. I part from you with feelings of love and affection; praying God's blessing upon you and the whole Church. Faithfully and affectionately your brother in Christ. Frank Page"

The Vestry replied graciously with a minute of appreciation which concluded, "For more than eleven years Mr. Page has gone in and out among this people, and, as a devoted pastor, an earnest faithful and true friend has made himself justly beloved.—The Vestry can only make record of his worth and service and of their esteem and affection. They offer him God speed in his new labors." The Rector went forth with almost one year's salary due him. It was finally paid in 1891.

THE REV. J. CLEVELAND HALL
COMES FOR A BRIEF MINISTRY

The Fairfax Courthouse Vestry requested July 1890 that Falls Church "join in a call to the Rev. J. Cleveland Hall of Manchester, a candidate for Holy Orders in this Diocese, at a salary of $600 per annum, one third to be contributed from Falls Church." The Falls Church approved effective Sept. 1, Mr. Nicolson says, "Mr. Hall was quite a scholarly man, who came into our ministry from that of the Presbyterian Church. He soon was asked to give a lecture to raise money for a charitable object. The Congregationalists loaned their church, the largest in the village. Mr. Hall took as his subject "Religion in Iron." He brilliantly compared Christians to cast iron, wrought iron and steel. (What a tribute that a teen-age boy should have been so impressed as to remember this subject when he was in his eighties.) Mr. Hall was here only a few months when he accepted a call to Danville, where he had a long ministry. His resignation was accepted with deep regrets.

THE FIRST TERM OF THE REV. ROBERT A. CASTLEMAN

The Vestry minutes for Dec. 5, 1892, read "The Rev. R.A. Castleman was living in Herndon but consented to give The Falls Church two Sunday afternoons a month. Students from the Seminary came on alternate Sunday afternoons. The second year the services were changed to the morning and the Vestry raised the annual salary to $350. By this time Mr. Castleman was also serving Langley and Vienna. The Vestry reported "Langley Church is ready to pay $300 toward the Rector's salary (We hope this was additional). Early in 1895 the Vestry invited Langley and Vienna "to elect three persons representative on the Vestry of The Falls Church." This Vienna did immediately.

Robert A. Castleman, an alumnus of the University of Virginia and Virginia Seminary, had also served in the Confederate Army. Nicolson says of him "I was confirmed under Mr. Castleman in a class of twelve, which we thought at that time was wonderful. Mr. Castleman had been a former teacher at the Episcopal High School, and his manliness made a strong appeal. I remember a teen-ager from Vienna saying to me as Mr. Castleman passed us, 'That is one member of the clerical profession I thoroughly respect.' In 1894 he started a baseball team and a chapter of the Junior Brotherhood of St. Andrew, when it was just coming into existence. Owing to the small population and rural character of Falls Church at that time, it was hard for us to find opportunities for service. We decided to assist the ladies of the congregation by hitching their horses to the wooden rails that stood where cars now drive in near the front of the church."

Mr. Castleman resigned in June of 1895 to accept a call to Bel Air, Maryland, and at the same time the minutes report "The Rector's salary is in arrears $121.14." It is pleasant to report, however, that the Vestry voted "to request $300 from the Diocesan Missionary Society to supplement the $700 pledged." We are glad that both amounts were forthcoming as reported at the July meeting when the minutes state, "Rev. Mr. Castleman's resignation accepted with resolution of regrets. Faithful pastor, earnest preacher, a true friend and helper of The Falls Church."

RECOLLECTIONS OF THE VILLAGE CHURCH

For many years, centering in the "gay nineties," The Falls Church was the Village Church around which grew the city of Falls Church. Realizing that members who knew that period still live among us, the author in 1959 asked several senior citizens to write for him their remembrance of The Falls Church about the turn of the century. Two excellent papers were given him, *Reminiscences of G.D. Gordon Nicolson* and *Recollections* by William Fitzhugh and Maud Morss Edmonds. The Rector herein expresses deep appreciation to them.

Mr. G.D. Gordon Nicolson, recently deceased, was a dear friend and vestryman. From 1909-1961 he served his parish in many ways. Nicolson Auditorium is named for him. The dedication plaque reads in part: "He served for 42 years as a Vestryman, for 34 years as Register and 25 years as Sunday School Superintendent."

The reminiscences of Mr. Nicolson have proven of inestimable value as a guide in writing large sections of this history. In his opening paragraphs he says:

"I think it may be well to start by telling you what our town was like when we came here in 1887.

It then extended from Haycock Road on the west to about where the Southern (Dulin) Methodist Church is on the east, on the north from a little beyond where Washington Street crosses the railroad to between Lee Highway and Arlington Boulevard on the south. The lots were large, some being of ten or twelve acres, and often having a cow, chickens and horse. During the Civil War the Federal troops had been through, many of whom later got positions under the Government in Washington and made their homes here. Therefore, we had more from New England and New York than from Virginia, nearly all of whom had high civic pride, resulting in the planting of trees and building of sidewalks even if no more than gravel. The population numbered about seven hundred, with an Episcopal, Roman Catholic, Northern (Crossman) Methodist, Southern (Dulin) Methodist Baptist, Presbyterian and Congregational churches. The latter had the largest building, being the one next to the present movie. However, it was the first and only one to go, most of its members joining the Presbyterian Church about the turn of the century. But the feeling of each body for the other was splendid, our town in this respect being thirty years ahead of most of the country, and this being especially so towards our Episcopal Church.

"On Broad Street there were not more than about six homes on each side between where the present bank is and the station at the west end of town. There were three post offices: Falls Church (near where the present bank is), West Falls Church, and East Falls Church. Finally, our population had a high proportion of collegians.

"When we came here in 1887, the State of Virginia was one diocese, with Bishop Whittle as head and Bishop Randolph (the first Bishop of Southern Virginia) as Assistant Bishop. He conducted the first confirmation I can remember with not more than three or four. Mr. Frank Page (a brother of Thomas Nelson) was then Rector, having also Fairfax Court House, and leaving here for Waco, Texas. He said Fairfax was seven miles in summer from Falls Church and ten in winter."

The delightful paper written by Mr. & Mrs. Edmonds is here given in full.

"At the request of our Rector, the Rev. J. Hodge Alves, we will endeavor to bring to you a picture of life and activities of The Falls Church as we knew it many years ago. We hope you will be able to visualize, as you look back over the years with us, the charm and serenity of this ancient building and the beauty of nature surrounding it.

In the 1890's, we were children in the Sunday School, and later, teenagers in the choir, and members of the Girls' Friendly Society and the Brotherhood of St. Andrew. At that time, the interior of the Church was quite crude, the flooring being of lumber furnished by the United States Government after the departure of the Union Army. The boards were of different widths and contained many knots—also knotholes. Our pitiful attempt to cover them resulted in one strip of somber carpet up the center aisle from door to chancel.

51

A chimney was built on the north side of the Church, when the Parker family discontinued the use of their summer kitchen and donated the bricks. If one looks carefully, the scars may be distinguished on the outside wall. Two huge stoves were set in boxes of sand, one on each side, and directly in line with the side door, the pipes being held by wires and suspended from the ceiling. Mr. John Lynch, the Sexton, built the fires on Saturdays and tended them carefully to be sure that the church would be comfortably heated for the three o'clock service on Sunday. The Vestryroom, made of flooring planks, occupied the south corner of the Church and was reached by the side aisle. The pews were of white pine, made by a local carpenter, and, as we remember they were most uncomfortable.

The churchyard was protected on the front and sides by a thick evergreen hedge, with three strands of barbed wire running through it. There was a heavy iron double gate at the entrance, made by Mr. W.N. Lynch, the village blacksmith. This was locked during the week. The walk leading to the Church was gravel and became very muddy at times. The maple trees on either side were given by Mrs. J. Frederick Huber, who, with her family, attended the church for many years. Honeysuckle grew in profusion back of the church, furnishing a barrier that discouraged intruders. Mr. Philip M. Edmonds, who was Junior Warden at the time, was designated "Captain" by the Rector; his duty was to summon the vestrymen to fight the honeysuckle in the church yard twice a year. They descended upon it with scythes, sickles, and rakes. After several days, they emerged the victors. The Reverend Dr. John McGill was our Rector at that time and Mr. Silas D. Tripp was our Sunday School Superintendent.

Our three Sunday School teachers were Miss Maud Hodgkin, Miss Jesse England, and Mr. George D. Nicolson. We thought them perfect, in spite of the fact we were often mildly rebuked for playing tag over the graves.

The outstanding event of our church year was Christmas. A huge tree was placed near the chancel and trimmed with glass icicles, strands of tinsel, strings of popcorn, and the traditional painted candy fruit. This candy was not supposed to be eaten, but how we longed to take just one bite! Our gifts were usually books, and for each child there was a small box of highly colored candy.

There were less than 300 residents in Falls Church at that time, so with five churches in town you can well imagine that the attendance in each was small. The first wedding ceremony performed in the Church after the Civil War was that of Selina M.

Slade and Philip M. Edmonds when The Reverend John McGill joined them in holy matrimony on October 25, 1877. In their old portfolio we found one of the first bulletins. Unfortunately, it has been mislaid so we can't recall who the Rector was at that time. However, we do remember that he was asking each member of the Church to increase his pledge to ten dollars a year, as it was becoming increasingly difficult to meet expenses.

On June 8, 1892, Mary Edwards Riley and Samuel Holmes Styles were united in marriage by The Reverend J. Cleveland Hall. Evidently, flowers played no part in church weddings at that time for the couple had to obtain special permission from the Bishop to decorate the Altar.

The day that Miss Mattie Gundry moved to Falls Church was a fortunate one for our Church. She bought the Schuyler Duryea house (situated on the present site of Tyler Gardens), and opened a school for mentally retarded children. She became quite active in the church and was a generous contributor, her first pledge being $50.00 a year. With her in our midst, we felt that our future was assured. It was due to her generosity that the unsightly boards that enclosed the vesting room were removed, and the red velvet curtains on brass rods were substituted. With our finances in better shape, it was decided that our next greatest need was a carpet. So many yards were bought and for many weeks the women, sitting on the floor, sewed strips together. At last the auspicious day dawned, and we proudly walked into the Church on red, wall-to-wall carpeting.

Miss Carrie Parker for many years gave of her strength and time to pump the old organ and direct the choir. Our lawn parties were very big events. All members attended with their entire families. All the men turned ice cream freezers while the women baked cakes and set up tables. The children put candles in the Japanese lanterns and the boys strung wires from which to hang them. These parties were usually held on Dr. Hodgkin's lawn. Perhaps many of you will remember his spacious old home on the hill, now the site of Tower Square shopping center.

Our next project was a cross for the altar. Mrs. James Oden, sponsor of the Girls' Friendly Society, offered the use of her side yard for the erection of a summer house in which to serve refreshments. The Vestry accepted, and for several summers the girls sold ice cream and cakes. At the same time, the Altar Guild and small groups of the Church women worked on their individual projects, so before too long, our goal was reached, and, with pride, we presented the cross that still adorns our altar.

Reminiscing is precious, and soon, the present congregation and future congregations who attend this beautiful old colonial Church will have their recollections, too."

CONCERNING SEMINARY STUDENTS

Mr. Nicolson writes, "At this point I will mention our deep appreciation for the work among us of seminary students, especially during the months between Rectors. Serving at this time were two who later became prominent: one was Mr. La Mothe who later was Rector of St. Paul's, the largest church in New Orleans; followed by a mission bishopric in Honolulu. The other was Robert Patton of Albermarle who was Rector of a large church in Pittsburgh and in 1918 took a leading part in establishing the Nation Wide Campaign which greatly strengthened the financial support of the whole Episcopal Church."

THE EYES OF THE VESTRY TURN AGAIN TO MCGILL

The same meeting of the Vestry that accepted Mr. Castleman's resignation, voted "to extend a call to the Rev. John McGill, of the Diocese of Southern Va.—extending to him the same financial support promised June 18 to Mr. Castleman." This support was a guarantee of $700 per year, with the hope that a further $300 could be gotten from the Diocesan Missionary Society. The minutes of the next meeting state: "That the Rev. John McGill accepted the call of the Vestry to become Rector of this Parish, his work to begin about Sept 15 '95 on terms recorded before."

Dr. McGill, for he had recently received an honorary Doctor in Divinity degree from Washington and Lee University, had been serving churches in Blacksburg, Virginia Polytechnic Institute, and at Christiansburg. His field of ministry was to include Langley and soon a new mission which he founded at Vienna. This mission grew rapidly and later became McGill Parish in honor of its founder. At first the McGills lived in a rented house, but soon moved into the first rectory on Oak Street.

Dr. McGill successfully guided the affairs of the Parish for over four years. The advance of the work was constantly limited by lack of finance, but the Rector quietly led the Vestry and congregation to stretch their sights. The envelope system was reintroduced, the Vestry agreed to reduce their asking of the Diocesan Missionary Society, the property and furnishings were insured for the first time and the Rector made up a correct register of members.

Dr. McGill quickly won the esteem and affection of the whole community, regardless of Church allegiance. He had a truly "ecumenical" spirit (long before this term was used) and worked untiringly for cooperation between the churches. Nicolson writes, "The first Good Friday three-hour service I ever attended was held by Dr. McGill. He had led all the ministers of our town, except the Roman Catholic, to participate at The Falls Church. At the conclusion of the hours, the bell of the Presbyterian Church was tolled."

The Spanish American War came during Dr. McGill's second tenure. Camp Alger was built on a large tract of land near Dunn Loring. Thirty thousand soldiers were in training there; and many attended services at The Falls Church. Mr. Nicolson writes, "There was shown to these men little of the hospitality so common during the two World Wars." They must have been better received at the church, for Mr. Nicolson told me that years later he greeted a stranger officer at church one winter Sunday. The man identified himself as a soldier who had often attended services during his training at Camp Alger and wished "to see the old church again."

In the fall of 1899 Dr. McGill was given a farm in Fauquier County near the Plains by his father-in-law, who was concerned for the health of both the Rector and his wife. He then tendered his resignation to the Vestry stating that he felt it best to retire to his farm. The Vestry unsuccessfully sought to dissuade him. He felt it would be unfair to The Falls Church for him to remain Rector and live on his farm.

He stated verbally (as later reported by Mr. Charles A. Stewart in his record) that " he had become deeply attached to the old church and the congregation, and it was with genuine regret that he tore himself away from its associations." Mr. Stewart added, "The Church gained both in spiritual and material growth during Dr. McGill's rectorship. At the time of his leaving the communicants had increased to seventy-five, in contrast to only twenty-one when he resigned only a few years before. Twenty-two families contributed regularly and thirty-two irregularly or not at all."

the falls church
in the
twentieth century

THE REV. GEORGE SOMERVILLE AND
THE SECOND LARGE RESTORATION

There have been four outstanding restorations of the time-honored colonial church. The first was under the devoted guidance of a layman, Captain Henry Fairfax, of whom it was said, according to a tablet placed on the church wall after his death, "But for his munificence this church might still be a ruin." The second was by the U.S. Army at the end of the War Between the States. The third was during the rectorship of the Rev. George S. Somerville, and the fourth and most extensive was in 1959.

The Vestry that accepted Dr. McGill's resignation with resolutions of deep regret immediately appointed a committee to seek a new Rector. At a joint meeting of the Vestries of Falls Church, Langley and Bailey's Cross Roads, November 13, 1899, the Register stated, "Correspondence with the Rev. George S. Somerville resulted in the acceptance by the latter of the call to the Rectorship of The Falls Church, the call being dated October 20, 1899, and offering him the sum of $900 to take charge of Falls Church, Langley and Bailey's Crossroads." This was increased to at least $1000 by the time of acceptance.

Mr. Somerville came from a successful rectorship in nearby Haymarket. Scarcely was the family settled in the rectory when dread diptheria took two of their children. Times were very hard for in September 1901 because of the financial situation of the Parish, the Rector was informed that for 1902 the Vestry could not guarantee more than $500 per annum in salary. The Treasurer's report at the end of 1901 showed receipts of $645.90 and expenditures of $629.29.

The new Rector organized the first vested choir at a time when such an organization could be found in Virginia only in large cities. He was a faithful pastor, visiting regularly on his horse, "Churchman." The two of them became a familiar sight on the roads around the village. Mr. Somerville is best remembered, however, for the restoration of the historic building which took place during his ministry. For some time the edifice had been badly in need of repairs. He at once determined to bring about a thorough restoration of the historic church, and at a Vestry meeting in July 1903 he presented his plan.

It was moved "that the Vestry sanctions the proposed improvements according to the design and plans submitted, provided money sufficient will be raised and placed in bank to fully cover all expense before work is begun." Realizing the limited means of the congregation, Mr. Somerville took the lead in raising funds in other areas. He turned especially to friends of his seminary days who now were rectors of strong parishes.

Mr. Nicolson says of his effort, "He was quite successful, raising enough money to replace the roof, floor and lower windows, using excellent materials and workmanship. A hot air furnace replaced the two stoves which had stood one on each side. The floor was raised in the East to form a chancel, and the two windows, one on each side, were converted to doors, leading into a vestry room where the present [1969] chancel now stands. A new chancel was given by the Daughters of Founders and Patriots of America."

This chancel filled the East end of the original church. It had a small altar that was against the East wall and stood on a platform. There was a brass rail around three sides. The chancel was divided with a clergy prayer desk and choir stalls on each side. The lectern and pulpit also stood on either side. There was a reredos of beautifully panelled wood. No attempt was made to follow the plan of the colonial interior, which probably was much like that of Pohick Church. The arrangement of the 1908 chancel was more in the Victorian than the Georgian tradition. A large portion of this chancel may be seen on the stage of the Gordon Nicolson Auditorium in the Parish House. The grounds were also improved by being leveled and seeded with lawn grass.

Mr. Somerville accomplished his purpose of fully repairing and beautifully doing over the interior of The Falls Church, but in doing so he overtaxed himself and undermined his health. He never recovered from an operation recommended by his doctors. He died in Clifton Springs, New York, March 4, 1908, just a few weeks before the contractors completed their work.

The Vestry and congregation were deeply grieved at the death of their Rector. Mr. J. Mitchell Smoot was appointed to represent the Vestry in assisting Mrs. Somerville in the arrangements necessary to bring back the Rector's body for burial in the churchyard. He was given $50 to take care of any expense. Mrs. Somerville was granted indefinite use of the Rectory. A warm letter of sympathy from the Ministers' Association of Falls Church signed by the Congregational and Presbyterian ministers as officers was sent to "The Old Falls Church."

Upon the occasion of the dedication of the new chancel November 9, 1913, the Senior Warden, S.D. Tripp, said of Mr. Somerville's work, "Like one inspired he set about the task of restoring the interior of this old church. He accomplished probably what no one else could have done at this time, and he laid down his life while strenuously working to preserve, improve and beautify the church he loved so well. It was he who brought the needs of our church to the attention of sympathetic friends. . .who so nobly responded to his appeal and generously furnished the means for this beautiful chancel."

The tablet presented by the Altar Guild which hangs on the North wall of the church says in part: "A noble man of noble ideals, he spent himself freely in the ministry of Christ and His Church. This restored colonial building is a fitting memorial to his patient zeal and inspiring devotion."

Most of 1908 was a strenuous time for the congregation of The Falls Church. There was sadness and joy of accomplishment and disappointment and hard work. There were five congregational meetings and the Vestry was called into session 23 times. Much needed to be done for the late Rector's family. A number of clergy declined to become Rector of "The Old Falls Church Episcopal Church" as it was regularly titled in the minutes. Yet much had to be done in completing the large work in the old building and in paying for it. Mr. Guy Camp, who had served as layreader and organist, had to resign because of pressure on his time.

THE REV. W. EDWARD CALLENDER BECOMES RECTOR

On October 19, 1908, the Rev. W.E. Callender, Rector of Epiphany Church, Laurens, South Carolina, accepted the call to be Rector. A native of Scotland, Mr. Callender emigrated to Norfolk, where he entered into the business of cotton exporting. He was deeply interested in the church and soon studied theology and was ordained a priest.

The Falls Church made much progress under this active and aggressive leader. Mr. Callender earnestly sought to bring people into the congregation; and at the Congregational meeting, Easter Monday, 1910, he reported "one hundred and thirty-two communicants, whose names are on the register." The meeting elected a Vestry of nine men. The tally sheet, signed by A. Wheeler, Jr., Secretary of the tellers, lists them with the votes received as follows: S.D. Tripp (29), C.A. Stewart (29), J.T. Unversaght (27), J.M. Smoot (22), C.A.S. Sinclair (25), H.A. Fellows (26), Gordon Nicolson (24), C.A. Marshall (27. P.D. Poston (18). The Vestry was organized into a number of committees, such as finance, building, grounds advisory and history.

The minutes report many activities. Night services were approved and ordered continued and the Rector officially thanked for his work. Permission was given for the formation of Langley Parish. For the first time a woman, Miss Mattie Gundry, was made Treasurer of the Church and invited to Vestry meetings.

A monthly news sheet called "The Falls Church Parish News" was mailed into the homes. This probably was the earliest forerunner of "The Bulletin of The Falls Church (Episcopal)." A copy for January 1910 is bound into the minutes. It lists officers and organizations: Rector, Rev. W. Edward Callender; Layreader, S.D. Tripp; Treasurer, Charles A. Marshall; Registrar, Harry G. Fellows; Superintendent of Sunday School, S.D. Tripp; Organist, Mr. E. Ballinger; The Falls Church Guild, Acting President, Mrs. Copper; St. Andrew's Brotherhood, Director, Gordon Nicolson; Falls Church Woman's Auxiliary, President, Mrs. Callender; Junior Branch, Directress, Mrs. Callender; Home Study Bible Class, Directress, Mrs. Foxwell; Daughters of The King, Directress, Miss Lillian Hunton.

Mr. Callender developed a strong interest in the outreach of the congregation. Trinity Chapel in the Arlington District was regularly ministered to, and early in 1910 a group from The Falls Church assisted the Rector in starting work at Farlee. Within a short time this became St. George's Chapel. The team from The Falls Church played the organ, ran the Sunday School and held services as layreaders.

"Before long," writes Gordon Nicolson, "so many members of the Chapel were there working that those from The Falls Church were no longer needed. A building was soon erected and the services were changed to Sunday mornings." Through the years a warm Christian relationship was continued between The Falls Church and her offshoot, St. George's.

The Rectory on Oak Street was in such poor condition that in October 1911 "the Vestry at Ballston" invited Mr. Callender to move into a rectory there. The Bishop approved the plan. The Vestry gave consent to this change and authorized the sale of the Oak Street property. The Vestry became increasingly dissatisfied with this arrangement. Therefore, one year later, October 1, 1912, it was resolved "that the Vestry of The Falls Church agrees that it will be to the best interest of the Church to have a resident minister. Believing that the present arrangement is detrimental to our church and unsatisfactory to the congregation, and after reviewing the situation carefully, and taking into consideration our Rector's successful work at Farlee, and looking to the best interest of both himself and the Church, it is deemed advisable not to renew the contract which terminates October 31, 1912." At a called meeting of the congregation on October 22 the Vestry resolution was read and overwhelmingly approved. The Vestry then asked for contributions toward the $126.45 due on the Rector's salary.

At a called meeting November 1, Mr. Tripp, treasurer, reported that he had sent the Rev. Mr. Callender the amount due him and had notified him no more salary would be paid. The Vestry approved and appointed a committee composed of Stewart, Styles and Nicolson to call on the Bishop. At a meeting two weeks later the committee reported they had seen the Bishop, and he had agreed to talk with the Rector about resigning.

The Rector tendered his resignation on November 5, 1912, whereupon the Vestry unanimously adopted the following resolution: "Whereas, our Rector, the Rev. W.E. Callender has tendered his resignation. . .therefore, be it resolved that the Vestry feels it necessary to accept Mr. Callender's resignation. . .and that we extend to him our best wishes for his continued success and assure him of our personal esteem."

THE REV. JOHN MCGILL, D.D. AGAIN RESPONDS

Several Priests declined the call of the Vestry, but finally with the approval of the Bishop, the Rev. John McGill was called once more at a salary of $70 a month and Rectory. Bishop Gibson wrote in part:

"I am glad to hear that you are not letting the work of the old church go down, but are doing the best you can for it. I shall be glad to license Dr. McGill as Missionary to The Falls Church and feel very comfortable indeed that you are in such good hands."

Dr. McGill agreed to serve until a regular Rector could be found. At the end of the six months he expressed pleasure at being given the opportunity to again serve the people of the congregation; and "to be allowed to go in and out among them all."

Mr. Stewart tells us that "Dr. McGill bore a striking resemblance to Gen. Robert E. Lee, of whom he was a great admirer. He told the writer that once he had the privilege of dining with General Lee while in camp. Bishop Johns had been invited and insisted that the young chaplain accompany him. The rough dining table with forked sticks for legs was covered with a clean white cloth, on which a choice leg of lamb was the appetizing dish. The General, said Dr. McGill, carved and served his guest with as much ease as if he had been surrounded by the luxuries of his own home."

Once again in the spring of 1917, Dr. McGill was to favor the congregation with his ministrations. He continued to live with his family on his farm in Fauquier County near The Plains, until the death of his wife, daughter of Colonel Beverley. He then lived with children in Washington, D.C., until, at the age of 86, he went on to join his beloved wife.

THE REV. ANDREW G. GRINNAN GIVES FOUR YEARS

On September 21, 1913, the Rev. Andrew Glassell Grinnan came from Haymarket, Virginia, to be Rector of The Falls Church. Mr. Grinnan was of distinguished Scotch ancestry and throughout his life corresponded with his kinsman, the Duke of Argyle, who while Governor General of Canada, visited him in his Rectory. After teaching for several years, Mr. Grinnan entered Virginia Seminary to study for the ministry. He served churches in West Virginia and at Haymarket. Just before coming to The Falls Church, ill health caused him to take a full year of rest.

His method of moving in those days was quite different from today as was the cost! In his letter of acceptance to the Vestry he wrote, "I have ordered a freight car for loading at Haymarket on the 12th and suppose that it will be in Falls Church by the 15th. The freight will be $23.00. My understanding is that I am to receive $70.00 a month—and the Vestry is to pay the freight on my things and move them from the car to the Rectory."

Nicolson writes, "Mr. Grinnan came to us with an energy and zeal limited only by a physical condition far below par. He used a bicycle as a conveyance and covered his territory remarkably well. Some Richmond relatives of his gave the money for improvements in plumbing and heating at the rectory, which added much to his comfort. He took the greatest interest in the Sunday School and procured a handprinting set, with which he added to our limited educational material. Among those confirmed under him was a little girl whose father was a nominal Episcopalian and mother a nominal Roman Catholic. She was at the child's Confirmation, saying to me at the conclusion, 'Mr. Nicolson, that was a beautiful service. I want to be confirmed and really take an interest in the church.' The family left soon after, but a few years later, I saw in the diocesan paper of Washington that former child was an assistant to the head of the children's department in one of the large Washington churches."

During his four years, in spite of his health, many fine things were accomplished and many interesting things happened. The Rectory was greatly improved with the help of funds from friends of the Rector. Brick walks were laid in the churchyard and electric lights were installed in the church. The Church Pension Fund was begun. After full discussion the Vestry voted unanimously to enter into this action by passing the following resolutions as recommended by the Church Pension Fund Committee:

"Resolved by the Vestry of the Parish of Falls Church, Virginia, that in obedience to the Canons of the General Convention and the Diocese of Virginia, this Parish accepts the assessment to assure support to the aged and disabled clergy and to the families of deceased clergymen, payable to the Church Pension Fund, which amounts to 7½ percent upon the salaries paid to the clergy connected therewith, being the sum of Twelve Hundred and twenty five dollars ($1225), and

"RESOLVED that the Treasurer of this Parish be and hereby is authorized to pay to the Treasurer of the Church Pension Fund Committee of the Diocese of Virginia, before March 1, 1917, one-twelfth of said amount of Ninety one 88/100 dollars ($91.88); and thereafter monthly payments of one-twelfth of said amount of $7.66, on or before the first day of each and every month.

"It is understood that these Resolutions are not to become effective unless and until the Church Pension Fund has completed the Reserve Fund of Five Million Dollars."

During these years the Parish lost two of its devoted members and Vestrymen and the community two of its finest citizens. One was Silas D. Tripp, who was Vestryman for thirty-five years. (This record was surpassed, however, by the Register who wrote of his death and was one of his pallbearers, G.D. Gordon Nicolson, who served 42 years.) The other was Dr. Louis Gott, a leading citizen and a trusted and beloved physician. He served on the Vestry for twenty years until failing health required his withdrawal, at which time he was made an honorary member.

The Rector had a sudden and critical paralytic attack just at Christmas 1916. He was taken to Richmond, where his brother, Dr. St. George Grinnan, was a leading surgeon. On Sunday morning, March 11, 1916, Andrew Grinnan, died at the age of 49.

The faithful friend of the congregation, the Rev. John McGill, again came to preach and hold services on Sunday mornings, travelling for two months from his home in Fauquier County for the last of his many ministrations to The Falls Church.

REV. ROBERT A. CASTLEMAN RETURNS TO COMPLETE A FULL MINISTRY

On May 20, 1917, the Vestry unanimously voted to recall the Rev. Robert Allen Castleman, Rector of Grace Church, Elk Ridge, Maryland, to again become their Rector. He accepted and served faithfully until his retirement fourteen years later. He, therefore, served The Falls Church longer than any other clergyman since colonial days. (Earlier, the Rev. Mr. Green, a son of the Parish, had served from 1737 to 1765.) Nicolson states, "Mr. Castleman came back to us in the summer of 1917 for a second term of duty. In spite of his advanced age and a most distressing illness in his family, he had here a most useful ministry."

During Mr. Castleman's ministry three former rectors were memorialized. Soon after his arrival an outstanding memorial service for the Rev. Andrew Glassell Grinnan was held in the Church. Addresses were given by the Rev. Samual A. Wallis, D.D., of Virginia Theological Seminary, The Rev. Frank Page of Fairfax, formerly Rector of The Falls Church, and the Rev. W.H. Burkhardt of Leesburg. The pastors of the Presbyterian Church, the Baptist Church, the Methodist Episcopal Church (North) and the Methodist Episcopal Church (South) were invited. Before he retired, both the Rev. Frank Page and the Rev. Dr. John McGill had died. They were warmly remembered by the Rector and Vestry. Words written by Mr. Castleman in one of the resolutions may be applied to all three priests: "The Falls Church is honored in having on the roll of its Rectors" the names of the Rev. Andrew Grinnan, the Rev. Frank Page and the Rev. John McGill.

First among the accomplishments of these years was the obtaining of the Church's first Parish House. Soon after Mr. Castleman's arrival an opportunity came to buy the old Baptist Church property on East Broad Street, which though not connected to the Church's property was near enough to be useful as a Sunday School room and Parish Hall. Nicolson, who was then Superintendent writes, "We had no Parish House, Sunday School being conducted under most trying obstacles in the Church. Where the present old Parish House is now (1959) was then occupied by a building that had been the Baptist Church, before their present stone building at Washington and Columbia. After the Baptists moved, the building was bought by a small group of people to be used as a Youth Center. This plan was not a success and the old building being vacant for several years, fell into great disrepair. We had long felt the need of a Parish Hall, with which Mr. Castleman heartily agreed. The joint owners, on learning of our need, offered to sell us the building and site for $500., a most generous offer. We bought it and finally put up the present wooden building, as the old building seemed not to fit our needs. The 1918 Nation-Wide campaign had made available some funds for the Diocese of Virginia to help needy churches. From this source we obtained $2,500 on condition that we raise $2,500. Mr. Merton E. Church, a deacon in the Northern Methodist Church, offered to give $500 or lend us $2,500 for three years without interest. We accepted the loan, tore down the old building and erected our present Parish House, which was completed in 1920. Later, we enlarged our facility by closing in and erecting classrooms on the ground floor and by better heating."

The Rectory in West Falls Church was rather inadequate, and Mr. Castleman desired to have his permanent home in Falls Church. The Vestry agreed to sell the Rectory and to give Mr. Castleman the income from the invested money. It was finally sold for $4,000.

A 1917 report of the Diocesan Committee on Clerical support, approved by Council, stated, "That it is the sense of the Council that the minimum salary for an unmarried clergyman should be $900.00, and that of a married clergyman $1,200.00, in addition to the rectory and Church Pension Fund provision, and that, in country parishes especially, the maintenance of a horse or car and the parish telephone be considered as a charge upon the parish." The Vestry agreed to meet this minimum and asked the Diocesan Missionary Society for further help. However, under the Rector's leadership the Parish soon relinquished this help and for the first time as a single congregation became fully self supporting.

During 1918 a minute of thanks was recorded "to Mr. Ryer for presenting to the church a tile or brick which was secured by him from the floor of the Episcopal Church in July 1864, the tile having been torn up by the Civil War soldiers and a number of them taken away by the soldiers as relics." This was probably the first of the original twelve tiles to be found or returned. Eight of these are now set into the sactuary floor under the Holy Table. A number were collected and presented to the church by Mrs. W. Leigh Ribble, wife of the former Rector.

To those of us who lived through the First World War a minute of the Vestry meeting November 1918 brings memories of one of the greatest epidemics of modern times: "The Church was closed by the town authorities during the month of October, due to the influenza epidemic."

That the congregation was growing and strengthening is indicated in the Annual Report of 1927, at the end of ten years of Mr. Castleman's Rectorate: Communicants 151, Confirmed Persons 203, Baptised Persons 283, Receipts for Fiscal Year $5,355.42; On Sunday School rolls 85, Teachers 2.

The Women's Guild presented to the Vestry at its meeting November 6, 1929, a report concerning the inadequacy of the church's facilities with regard to: 1.) Insufficient heat in the Church; 2.) No Rectory; 3.) Parish Hall too small and badly placed.

They requested that the Vestry formulate a plan to provide for the future concerning these matters. A committee was appointed to consider the substance of this petition composed of Mrs. J.T. Unverzaght, Mr. R.H. Lane and Mr. C.A. Stewart. Thus began the effort to build adequate Parish Hall facilities adjacent to the Church and to provide a worthy Rectory. It was 30 years before the need was adequately met.

Times were hard as the Great Depression grew and the life of the Parish seemed to reflect this gloom. The total receipts for 1930 were only $3,227.23.

At the meeting of the Vestry July 1, 1931, Mr. Castleman stated that he felt the time had come for him to retire, and he therefore presented his resignation as Rector of The Falls Church to become effective after the next Sunday, July 5. On the 6th the Vestry voted a resolution of appreciation, stating that the Rector, having passed the retirement age and having seen fit to present his resignation as Rector of The Falls Church, the Vestry had accepted the resignation effective July 6, and that the Vestry "unanimously expresses its deep appreciation of Mr. Castleman's loyal support and untiring efforts in connection with this historic old church, covering the period from July 1, 1917—with deep regret that this separation has become necessary, the Vestry expresses the hope—that God's richest blessing will rest upon Mr. Castleman and his family."

THE REV. CLARENCE S. MCCLELLAN IS CALLED

On January 3, 1932 on invitation of the Vestry, the Rev. Clarence Stuart McClellan preached at 11 a.m. to a full church. That afternoon, the Vestry was called into special session at the home of the Junior Warden, C.A. Stewart. On statement that the large congregation had been highly pleased with the preacher, the Vestry voted unanimously to call Mr. McClellan to be Rector. The salary was set at $2,100 and a rectory to be built by May 1, 1932. The Register was instructed to write Bishop Tucker for his permission to extend this call. Bishop Tucker gave his approval, and on January 19 the Vestry issued a call to Mr. McClellan to become Rector July 1, 1932. He accepted the call on January 14.

Mr. McClellan was born in New York City of Scotch-Irish parents, and he was educated at New York University and Cornell University. He received his theological training at Union Seminary, New York. In addition, he had served churches in New York, Connecticut, Maryland and Texas before going to North Carolina. His flamboyant career included preaching to the Indians and cowboys of the West, touring Asia, Europe and Africa and what he considered "his crowning work," the founding of "The Open Air Westminster Abbey of the South" at Calvary Church in Fletcher, North Carolina.

The Rector-elect was invited to speak and lead The George Washington Bicentennial service on Feb. 21, 1932. The Church was filled to overflowing with many distinguished persons in the congregation. The Choir of All Saints,' Chevy Chase, Maryland, with 40 trained voices and eight trained soloists, led the music. The complete service was broadcast over the Columbia Network from WJSV.

The McDaniel home, an attractive two-story frame dwelling in the triangle at Fairfax and Broad Streets, was purchased for the Rectory at a cost of $9,000. The McClellans with their four boys moved into it on arrival.

The congregations were large. Mr. McClellan reported an average of 122 for eight Sundays. The Laymen's League, said to be the first in the Diocese of Virginia, was organized to bring the men together. The Rector's Discretionary Fund was established. Messrs. Charles A. Stewart and Samuel H. Styles were appointed to the Board of Trustees of Oakwood Cemetery Association. [This is a non-profit corporation managed by the Trustees composed of two representatives from each of the five Protestant churches in the town at that time, i.e.; Baptist, Episcopal, Presbyterian and Dulin and Crossman Methodist churches.]

On September 5, 1931, Mr. McClellan resigned for reasons of health. The Wardens announced that the Rev. Malcolm S. Taylor, of the College of Preachers, Washington Cathedral, and a resident of Falls Church, had consented to arrange for services during the vacancy in the rectorship. Bishop Tucker advised that a Rector be called promptly and offered his assistance.

The Two Hundredth Anniversary of the establishment of The Falls Church was celebrated November 25, 1934. Many Government officials including The President of the United States, the Governor of Virginia and the Mayor of Falls Church, editors of all area newspapers, the Bishops of Virginia and the clergy of the area were invited. The President and Mrs. Franklin D. Roosevelt sent flowers for the altar with personal regrets. Governor George C. Percy also sent his regrets. The *Washington Herald* reported, "The Rt. Rev. Henry St. George Tucker, Bishop of Virginia; the Rev. Dr. G. McLaren Brydon, historiographer of the Diocese of Virginia; and many other leading divines of Virginia and Maryland were present. The ancient place of worship was filled to overflowing."

Two special services were held. At eleven o'clock in the morning the Rev. Malcolm S. Taylor was in charge of the service. The Rt. Rev. Henry St. George Tucker, Bishop of Virginia, was the preacher. At 3:30 p.m. the Rev. R.A. Castleman, former Rector, led the service of Evening Prayer and Dr. Brydon gave the historical address.

Following Mr. McClellan's resignation, the Church was without a Rector for eight months. At the Annual Meeting of the congregation January 7, 1935, the Senior Warden, Mr. Charles A. Stewart, presided. He reported that the Vestry had consulted with leaders of all organizations "as to the kind of Rector to be sought" and had found them to be in agreement with the Vestry's ideas. The names of thirty-one clergy had been presented to the Vestry for consideration, all of whom had been discussed and inquired about. Many of these had been interviewed and some had conducted services.

A report of a Committee on the Terms of Vestrymen was opposed to the idea of rotation, with one third elected each year for a term of three years. The report stated, "This is inadvisable because it makes it impossible to change the complexion of the Vestry at any election". . .and "automatic retirement based solely on length of service is unintelligent and indiscriminating." The resolution to change was defeated.

YEARS OF GROWTH UNDER RIBBLE

The Rev. Watkins Leigh Ribble became the Rector of The Falls Church on March 10, 1935. Mr. Ribble had preached for the congregation, on invitation of the Vestry, the Sunday after Christmas. The letter issuing the call states: "At a regular meeting of the Vestry of The Falls Church, on Feb. 6th, 1935, you were by unanimous vote of all seven members elected Rector of this Parish. The salary is $1800 a year and rectory. We are anxious for you to take charge as soon as you conveniently can."

In his letter of acceptance Mr. Ribble said, "I look forward with pleasure to becoming rector of your parish, hoping that I might measure up to the opportunities for service I feel that Falls Church presents."

Mr. Ribble was 35 years of age. He and his wife Constance had three children. He was born in Brazil to missionary parents. His father, a native of Wytheville, Virginia, was in charge of missions of the Episcopal Church in that country. Leigh following in his father's footsteps, upon graduation from Virginia Seminary in 1927, was sent as a missionary back to Brazil, the land of his birth. At the time of his election to The Falls Church Mr. Ribble was a missionary in the Archdeaconry of the Blue Ridge and in charge of Grace Church, Stanardsville, Virginia, and six other missions.

Mr. Stewart, writing after five years of Mr. Ribble's rectorship, states, "He is earnest and enthusiastic in his work, and upon taking charge both he and Mrs. Ribble became at once very popular with the parishioners, young and old. . .During this five and a half years the church has prospered perhaps as never before, both spiritually and materially. He has done a splendid work in building up interest in this old historic church and the large attendance is ample testimony to the good work he is doing in the parish. The records show an increased roll of communicants, and attendance at church services as far ahead of previous years. . .The church, parish hall and rectory are now in excellent condition. The communicants at this year end number 341 and baptised members 457. . .The Church School now enrolls 142."

Soon after Mr. Ribble arrived, his predecessor, the Rev. Robert A. Castleman, died and was buried from the church with most impressive ceremonies. The Rt. Rev. Henry St. George Tucker, Bishop of Virginia, and the Rector were in charge of the service. The press stated that it was the largest funeral ever held in The Falls Church.

One of the unusual events of these years was the ordination of Temple Goode Wheeler to the ministry of the Church. His family were active in The Falls Church. On July 26 the Vestry certified that, "we believe that Temple G. Wheeler, for the past three years, hath lived a sober, honest and godly life—and think him worthy to be admitted to the Sacred Order of Deacons." He was ordained to the diaconate by the Rt. Rev. Frederick D. Goodwin in December 1936 and to the priesthood by Bishop Strider of West Virginia in March 1938. He has spent his whole ministry in the faithful shepherding of small missions and in work with boys and girls in the Diocese of West Virginia. Before ordination Temple Wheeler was a devoted member of The Falls Church and assisted in its youth program. He has continued to visit the parish and to assist with preaching or services.

As the congregation grew, the Rector found need of more assistance in his large work. Mr. Ribble again turned to the Virginia Seminary and brought into the parish a succession of fine men, who were studying for the ministry. This happy relationship with the Seminary has continued through the years. Mr. Ribble was also assisted by several retired clergy who lived in this part of Virginia. One who served for a long period and in many ways was the Rev. John G. Sadtler, retired, who had his home in Falls Church.

The congregation was growing steadily in every area. Mr. L.W. Harrison, as chief usher, made regular reports which showed that generally attendance was increasing. The congregation, however, used to a small town church, had difficulty in lifting its sights to the great needs and opportunities of this new day.

The Rector's salary was not in line with the advancing cost of living. As the war years wore on, this became so evident that in 1943 a resolution presented by the Wardens, Messrs. Charles A. Stewart and Harold J. Spelman, was unanimously adopted, "In view of the increased cost of living, it is ordered that an additional compensation of $300 per year be paid to the Rector, the Rev. W.L. Ribble, effective July 1st, and continuing during the war emergency."

As the parish grew the Rector's time was divided more and more. He strongly presented his need for secretarial assistance. Sixteen dollars a month was provided for this purpose, but not until several years after the war did the parish provide a regular secretary. The need for more adequate space was regularly presented by the Rector, the Sunday School and other organizations, but it was after Mr. Ribble had left the parish that additional space was provided by the building of vestry rooms at the East end of the Church.

From 1941 the United States was involved in the war that was being waged all over the world. The Falls Church was not directly involved, but many of her members were. Offerings were taken for the Relief of British Churches, for the Army and Navy Chaplains Fund and for the Red Cross (which was allowed regular use of the Parish House). The congregation joined at times in transporting and entertaining G.I.'s. Efforts were made to counteract the decrease in attendance caused by the rationing of gasoline and tires, by setting up car pools. The Rector, as Air Raid Warden, on several occasions gave instructions to the congregation.

The spiritual life was strengthened by the addition of more regular services, by special Lenten evenings with outstanding speakers and by the organization of both Junior and Senior Chapters of the Brotherhood of St. Andrew and an active Altar Guild. The congregation, under the leadership of the Rector and General R.H. Lane, Chairman, entered into the National "Forward In Service" Program. As early as 1942 a United Good Friday service was held in The Falls

Church, indicating the early interest of the Rector and The Falls Church in "ecumenical" efforts. There were also some difficulties and disappointments and hardships, as is always true in any live work.

In February 1945 Mr. Ribble resigned as Rector to become the Rector of Grace and Holy Trinity Church, Richmond, Virginia. The Resolutions that the Vestry unanimously adopted are a fitting tribute to the effective and fruitful ministry of this good priest and rector. They also attest to the quality of the relationships between Pastor and People. In part they said:

"WHEREAS Reverend Watkins Leigh Ribble is leaving The Falls Church on April 6, 1945, after more than ten years as rector; and WHEREAS the Reverend Mr. Ribble came to the parish when its morale was low and its affairs were in confusion; and—by his initiative, energy, executive ability and sound leadership, elevated the morale of the parish and replaced confusion by order and efficiency;—

"The Vestry, on behalf of the people of the parish, express to Mr. and Mrs. Ribble their profound regret that the happy association of the past ten years is to be terminated, and hearty wishes for their happiness and success in their new field of work; and tender to Mr. and Mrs. Ribble expression of heartfelt gratitude for their splendid leadership and for the inspiration of their example of loving Christian service."

At the Annual Meeting before his resignation, Mr. Ribble had given a statistical report that indicates the strong growth made by the congregation during the ten years of his ministry: Baptisms 238, Confirmations 200, Services 1565, Communicants 452 (was 186 in 1935), Income $10,101 (was $4,085 in 1935).

As the Grace Church resolution had prayed in 1935, "Physical strength, mental power and the Grace of God had combined to bless his undertaking." The Ribbles gave to The Falls Church a goodly ministry.

AN INTERIM PERIOD

Simple but effective plans were made to carry on the regular life of the Parish. Seminarians and nearby clergy were asked to help on a regular basis. Outstanding among those men studying for the ministry was Joseph Horn, a candidate for holy orders from the Diocese of Alabama. He began with Mr. Ribble and continued under Mr. Hayes. Of him, Mr. Hayes writes, "At the beginning of my ministry in The Falls Church, I inherited from my predecessor a seminary student, Joseph Horn from Alabama, who contributed a tremendous amount both to the life of the congregation and to my own ministry."

71

During this period news came to the Vestry and congregation that Mrs. Julien Russell, recently deceased, had left a legacy estimated to be at least $10,000. The income was to be used for the care of the colonial church and its grounds. This was the largest legacy The Falls Church had ever received.

After consultation with Bishop Goodwin and friends among the Seminary Faculty, the Vestry appointed committees of Visitation who traveled to a number of churches both in and out of the Diocese. The choice centered on the Rev. Francis W. Hayes, Jr., Canon of the Cathedral of The Incarnation, Garden City, L.I., New York. The Vestry unanimously voted "That the Wardens are instructed to offer the Rev. Francis W. Hayes a formal call to be Rector of this Parish." After a visit of Mr. and Mrs. Hayes and discussion with them, the salary was set at $3300, rectory and travel.

HAYES' RECTORSHIP FACES POPULATION EXPLOSION

On July 1, 1945, the Rev. Francis W. Hayes, Jr., became the Rector of The Falls Church. He was born in Rhode Island, but had spent much of his life in Texas, from whose University he was a graduate. He also held a Bachelor in Divinity degree from Virginia Seminary and had done graduate study at General Theological Seminary, New York. Mr. Hayes had served two churches in Houston, Texas, before going to the Cathedral in Long Island. His wife was born Jeannette Louise Ervin. They had two children. (Their twins were born while they lived in Falls Church.)

The following notes on his years in The Falls Church were graciously prepared by Mr. Hayes at the author's request. We are grateful for them and are glad to be able to publish them.

"I went to Falls Church in the early summer of 1945 between the end of the war in Europe and the end of the war in Japan. Falls Church at that time was still a relatively sleepy Virginia town, but just becoming aware of the influx of outsiders working for the Government, who were not Virginians. The church was a good-sized congregation, but still with small church background and ideas. Only in the congregational meeting prior to my coming had the hold of the old-timers upon the Vestry been partially broken and some of the newer people elected to the Vestry. Also, at that early 1945 congregational meeting the idea of Vestry rotation was instituted, but this did not include the officers!

"Mr. John Conway Henry was ordained Deacon in The Falls Church on July 25, 1947, by the Rt. Rev. Frederick D. Goodwin, Bishop of Virginia. He was presented by the Rector, and the Rev.

W. Leigh Ribble was the preacher. He and his wife, Elizabeth Rhea (Preston), had taught in the Sunday School and served as Youth Counsellors. Mr. Henry was the third son of the congregation to enter the ministry since the War Between the States. He continued his studies at Virginia Seminary, where he received his B.D. degree in 1948. He was ordained Priest in June 1948 by the Rt. Rev. W.R. Mason, Suffragan. Mr. Henry has served churches in Virginia and has returned to preach in The Falls Church.

"The war ended shortly after the beginning of my rectorship and contrary to the ideas of some pessimists on the Vestry, Falls Church did not become a ghost town as predicted, but rather began its boom, which has continued in the surrounding areas even down to the present time. The whole nature and complexion of the community and the church changed during the ensuing years. More and more people came in, the congregation became predominantly transient and military. At the height of this growth we estimated in the church office that we were adding 250 families a year to our mailing list, and subtracting 225.

"During this almost twelve-year period of my rectorship there was quite a bit of physical expansion in the church due to the rapid growth of the congregation. Immediately following the relaxation of restrictions on building at the end of the war, the 1905 "temporary" vestry room of clapboard was removed and a more adequate brick addition made to the east end of the church. In 1950-51 the parish house immediately behind the church building was constructed, which for the first time brought the church school and social life of the congregation into immediate proximity with the church building and its worship services. Prior to that time the old frame parish house on East Broad Street had been the sole means of housing the church school that was growing by leaps and bounds and an ever-increasing social program and organizational outreach in the congregation. In 1953 with the widening of East Broad Street and East Fairfax Street the old rectory at the apex of the triangle, which has the church at one corner and the center of town at the other, was made most inadequate and inefficient, as indeed it had been for many years, and a new modern rectory was built in the Broadmont section of town.

"In 1956 and 1957 with the still expanding congregation and community, the existing church building proving most inadequate for the size of our membership, steps were taken to provide more adequate facilities for our worshipping life. A financial campaign was undertaken with the idea in mind of building a new church. This financial campaign, conducted with professional help, was most successful. The idea at that time was to keep the old church building parallel to the parish house, fronting on Fairfax Street. It was on these assumptions that the campaign was held and made successful.

"During this period in the early and middle fifties with the obvious needs of the growing congregation requiring more space within which to expand, land was purchased behind the old parish house on Broad Street and immediately behind the church property. This totally enclosed half acre provided more immediate contact with the old parish house so that there was communication between the two buildings. Later in that decade, property was purchased to the east of the parish house, which included the old Wheeler home, one of the older Falls Church families and members of the congregation.

"Organizationally, the most significant events of that twelve-year period were the combination and reorganization of existing women's groups into a unified plan for the churchwomen, and the creation of a fine large churchwomen's group with ten circles or guilds. Also reorganized in the middle fifties was the Brotherhood of St. Andrew, which became a strong force among laymen. The Women of the Church soon organized the Thrift Shop as a ways and means project.

"Part of the expanding and ongoing life of The Falls Church has always been the personnel who have been affiliated and who have worked with it. Outstanding among the seminarians were Joseph Horn (mentioned earlier), Lee Graham and Joe Pinder. Then there was a series of clerical assistants: The Rev. Dabney Wellford, now of Warsaw, our first deacon assistant. He served well until he left us to become the vicar of, and first rector of, St. Patrick's Church in Jefferson Village. I might add that it was during this period that St. Patrick's was begun. Following Dabney, Charles Horn, brother of Joe, came to us from the seminary as a lay person, not having finished his degree of work at the seminary, nor having passed his canonicals; and as a layman, was with us for a year. At the time of his ordination to the diaconate, we also added another deacon to the staff in the person of Louis Bradford. During this same period we had the assistance of an Army chaplain, the Rev. Kenneth Sowers, who was stationed at the Pentagon, and who gave us much of his free time and proved quite able, helpful and quite beneficial to the parish. This was the set-up when I resigned in the spring of 1957.

"Speaking of people, I would not omit the contribution of Percy H. Burness, who served so long as our organist and choir director.

Following him, our own member, Donald Mori, continued the fine musical traditions he had inherited.

"Lay leaders, who are no longer with us, but whose memory still is, would include especially Charles E. Stewart, Senior Warden; Samuel Styles, Treasurer; and Albert Lester, Vestryman.

"Along with the creation by our congregation of St. Patrick's Church, we also cooperated with St. Mary's, Arlington, and St. John's, McLean, in the establishment of St. Dunstan's Church, where Grant Sherk now is. I had the most immediate charge of its beginnings, taking communion there monthly.

"During this expanding period in our community the church felt the same growth, with Church School enrollments exceeding all others in the Diocese, and baptisms and confirmations doing the same."

The high water mark for the number of persons involved in The Falls Church came in 1956; baptisms, 104; confirmations 182; baptised persons, 2629; communicants 1261; and in the Sunday School, 883 with about 100 teachers and workers. This was the year that saw four clergy active in the congregation (the only time in all history that The Falls Church had that many). This year also saw another congregation, St. Dunstan's, organized in what had been The Falls Church area, bringing the number of new churches in its area to three. At the same time the population wave was moving farther out into Fairfax County. Therefore, there began in 1957 the slow recession in numbers, which has continued, but in 1969 is slowly stabilizing.

The pressure for a larger church and more adequate parish house facilities was mounting. Already four services were scheduled for Sunday mornings at 7:30, 8:30, 10 and 11:30, and there were often duplicate services in the auditorium, especially at the great seasons. There were full Sunday Schools at 8:30, 10 and 11:30. The Annual Meeting of the congregation Jan. 11, 1956, authorized the building of a new church and the set up of a special campaign for raising the funds for this program.

The Committee to plan for the new church: Dr. Randal Robertson, Chairman, Messrs. Cabell Busick, Robert Hubbell, Thomas Pringle, Junior Warden, Harold Spelman, Senior Warden, and the Rector was already laying plans for this undertaking.

In May 1956 the Financial Campaign was organized with the guidance of the Wells Organization. Mr. Donald E. Ball was General Chairman, Mr. Jon Roan, Special Gifts Chairman, Mr. A.O. Woolridge, Teams Chairman, and Mrs. Sidney Hinds, Dinner Chairman. Five hundred members attended the dedication and kick-off dinner at George Mason Junior-Senior High School. By the end of the year pledges totalling $250,245.50 had been obtained from 665 families. The New Church Committee began the search for an architect. They set "two prime qualifications: (1) He should have had considerable experience with Virginia colonial architecture as applied to churches and, (2) he should have an understanding and feeling for the Episcopal Church." A number of architects were studied and several were interviewed. Mr. Milton L. Grigg of Charlottesville and Alexandria was selected and agreed to be the architect for the new church. Mr. Grigg, an active Episcopalian, had graduated from the University of Virginia and had been a member of the group who worked on the Williamsburg restoration. He was a member of the Architectural Commission of the Diocese of Virginia and a recognized authority on colonial churches. Mr. Grigg and his associates set to work immediately to prepare plans for the large development.

At a meeting called by the Rector, April 2, 1957, the Rev. Francis W. Hayes, Jr., presented to the Vestry his resignation as Rector of The Falls Church to be effective May 1.

"This is to present my resignation as Rector of The Falls Church, effective April 30, 1957.

"As most of you are aware, St. Timothy's Church, Catonsville, Maryland, extended a call to me to become their Rector some weeks ago. That call as most of you may have heard was declined. They have in this past week renewed their call to me, and after further deliberation and much prayer, I have decided to accept it.

"Having been Rector of this old and beloved Church for almost twelve years does not make this decision easy. Having been so closely associated with so many of you for these many years, makes this decision doubly difficult. I am sure that there will be many moments of doubt in times to come as to whether this was the proper course to take. One does not uproot firm foundations without some strain. I hope you will all pray with me that this is done with the guidance of the Holy Spirit, and that His work may be furthered by this move."

At a special meeting of the Vestry on April 10, the following resolution was passed unanimously:

"BE IT RESOLVED—That, in its own behalf and that of the Congregation of The Falls Church, the Vestry, even as it accepted Mr. Hayes' resignation with deepest regret, hereby extends to him the most sincere and heart-felt gratitude for the innumerable benefits that the years of his ministry, given so unstintingly, have brought to The Falls Church and to the community; and hereby expresses to Mrs. Hayes warm appreciation for the vital part contributed to all concerned by her friendship, patience, and understanding; and hereby conveys to The Reverend Francis W. Hayes, Jr., to Mrs. Hayes, and to each of their children, all of the very best wishes for the good health, happiness and success which, by God's grace, we pray shall be theirs to enjoy wherever they may be in the years ahead."

The Register was instructed to have this resolution printed in the Church Bulletin and to send copies to the Bishops of Virginia and the Bishop of Maryland.

A BUSY YEAR FOR THE VESTRY

It was more than a year before The Falls Church had a Rector. The leadership fell heavily upon the Senior Warden and Vestry. During this period there were two meetings of the congregation and thirty-three meetings of the Vestry. Not only did they have to find a successor to Mr. Hayes, but also to continue the work of planning for the desperately needed buildings and carry the administrative load of a large and active church. Their loyalty, concern and constant "care of the church" is worthy of praise. The congregation at its 1958 annual meeting expressed warmly its appreciation to the Senior Warden and the Vestry.

In June, just before the new Rector took over, the Vestry expressed the feelings of all in a special resolution of thanks to the Senior Warden. ". . .Mr. Harold J. Spelman with unstinting devotion, has. . . given excellent leadership, wise counsel and patient cooperation . . .The Falls Church expresses to Mr. Spelman love and gratitude, and for his dedication to our fellowship, gives thanks to Almighty God."

The spiritual leadership fell to Chaplain Sowers and the two young Deacons. However, in June 1957, the Chaplain withdrew from his part-time work. A resolution of warm appreciation from the Vestry said in part, "Whereas, Kenneth M. Sowers, Chaplain (Col.), U.S. Army. . .has served with the clergy of The Falls Church from September 1955. . .The Vestry, in its own behalf and that of the congregation, extends to Chaplain Sowers warm and heartfelt gratitude for his many contributions to the life of this parish."

Saturday, June 8, 1957, The Reverends Louis Munroe Bradford, Charles Kettler Horn and Spencer Records Quick were ordained to "The Sacred Order of Priests" in The Falls Church by The Rt. Rev. Robert F. Gibson, Bishop Coadjutor of the Diocese of Virginia. The Rev. Frank Hayes preached and presented the two young Deacons of the Parish.

With Mr. Horn as senior, these two young priests carried on the leadership of the spiritual life of The Falls Church until a Rector was obtained. Along lines worked out between them, with the help of the Senior Warden, they divided the spheres of teaching, preaching and all priestly functions. At the 1958 Annual Meeting, the Senior Warden said, "I know that I speak for all when I express my appreciation for. . .the devoted and untiring services of Mr. Horn and Mr. Bradford. We have seen them increase day by day in 'wisdom and ghostly strength.' "

Mr. Horn resigned on May 15, 1958, to become the Rector of the Church of the Epiphany, Guntersville, Alabama. Words of the Vestry bespeak the esteem of all: "Whereas, in a situation complicated by the absence of a Rector, Mr. Horn has served with competence, warmth and devotion, in behalf of itself and the congregation, the Vestry extends to the Rev. Charles K. Horn the most sincere and heartfelt gratitude."

The Rev. Louis M. Bradford became the Senior Curate and spiritual head of the congregation. His willingness to accept the invitation of the incoming Rector to remain with him and the parish for a full year was a blessing to all.

One other noteworthy event took place during this period: November 3, 1957 the congregation celebrated the 225th anniversary of its founding with a special Service of Thanksgiving. The Bishop of Virginia, the Rt. Rev. Frederick D. Goodwin, the Coadjutor, the Rt. Rev. Robert F. Gibson and the Curates conducted the service. The Rev. Francis W. Hayes gave the historical address. Many notables and a large congregation filled the Church.

The Senior Warden, immediately on the resignation of the Rev. Mr. Hayes, had appointed a Preliminary Inquiry Committee "to obtain and receive names of possible successors to Mr. Hayes, to evaluate relevant, available data concerning them, and to report thereon to the Vestry." This committee was composed of Mr. Robert Hubbell, Chairman, Mesdames J.L. Harrison and L.W. Harrison, General Sidney Hinds, Dr. Randal Robertson and Messrs. James McBroom, Albert Lester, Jerome Shay, Harold Spelman, Senior Warden, and Thomas Pringle, Junior Warden. Through a year of work this committee held many meetings, alone and with the Vestry, and made many visits to churches in Virginia and other dioceses. They conferred with the Bishops, seminary professors and many other friends. They prepared lists and dossiers and made studies of some fifty clergymen. Five who were chosen declined.

THE FALLS CHURCH CALLS JOSEPH HODGE ALVES

On January 7, 1958, after reports from Dr. Randal Robertson and General Sidney Hinds, who had visited Christ Church, Little Rock, Arkansas, and the report of the committee who had met with Bishop Robert Brown of Arkansas, "The Vestry by unanimous vote decided to extend a call to the Rev. Joseph Hodge Alves to become Rector of The Falls Church." On January 8, the Senior Warden wrote, extending the formal call and inviting Mr. and Mrs. Alves to visit the church before making a decision.

"Ours is an old church which has experienced a large growth in recent years. We now have 1200 communicants—our Bishops describe the work as a great challenge—The salary of the Rector is $9,500 plus use of the Rectory and travel allowance—We would like to have you and your wife know us and see our church and community."

After a visit to The Falls Church and much study of the ministry involved, Mr. Alves decided to decline the call. Bishop Goodwin, with whom he had worked as a Seminarian, asked him to fly to Virginia and discuss his reasons with the Vestry. Bishop Gibson, the Coadjutor, arranged for another meeting with the Vestry. Mr. Alves told them his concerns were the uncertainty concerning the large building program, and his inability to feel the strong support from the Vestry and congregation that would be needed for so large a work. The Vestry minutes of February 5 read, "Mr. Alves then indicated that the result was to clarify these matters and to give him a better understanding. . .In brief he related that an around-the-table discussion of this kind was, in his opinion, a very important procedure in connection with the calling of a Rector: The Vestry then by unanimous vote of all members present, extended to Mr. Alves a second call to become Rector. To this the Bishop agreed."

On February 7, 1958, Mr. Alves telegraphed his acceptance to the Senior Warden. The minutes of the Vestry and The *Bulletin* gave a rather full biography of Mr. Alves. The following is a summary:

Joseph Hodge Alves, Jr., was born January 4, 1905, in Henderson, Kentucky, of families who had come from Scotland and England to colonial North Carolina and Virginia. He was brought up in Alabama, and educated at the University of the South, Sewanee, Tenn., B.A. 1926, and Virginia Seminary, B.D. 1929. He had been Rector of Christ Church, Little Rock, Arkansas, for nine years. Before that he was Rector of St. Paul's, Mobile, Alabama; St. Paul's, Lubbock, Texas; and St. James, Alexandria, Louisiana. He also organized missions in each of these areas. He had been active in the affairs of the community and the whole church throughout his ministry. At the time of his call he held positions in the Boy Scouts, Red Cross, Health and Welfare Council and the Ministerial Association, which he had helped to integrate. He was President of the Standing Committee, Deputy to General Convention, Chairman of Promotion and Provincial Chairman of Christian Education. He and Mrs. Alves, nee Josephine Fry of New Orleans, had three daughters and one son, all teenagers.

Mr. Alves set the date of acceptance as June 15 in order that his children could finish their school year and that he might present, as their Rector, two of his youth who were to be ordained deacons in Christ Church, June 11.

On June 22, 1958, the Rt. Rev. Frederick D. Goodwin, Bishop of Virginia, officially instituted Mr. Alves as the Rector of The Falls Church. The Rev. Alfred St. John Matthews, Rector of St. John's, McLean, was preacher. A *Bulletin* article at that time said, "The Rev. Mr. and Mrs. J. Hodge Alves, and JoAnn, Betsy, Amelia and Hodge were guests at a beautiful reception given to introduce them to the Congregation on the afternoon of June 29. A large portion of the Parish Family attended."

The Rector found there was no summer lull. He immediately set to work calling on the sick and seeking to understand this large complex parish. It was decided to continue the heavy schedule of four Sunday morning services, as attendance remained large. Leaders and representatives of all groups and activities were called to a half-day meeting, of which the Church Secretary and *Bulletin* Editor, said "Our Planning Session was three hours well spent. Leaders of all church organizations learned what each is doing—and plans were made and co-ordinated for the future. Neither stifling heat nor violent thunder storm ruffled the feeling of unity and keen interest at this— our first assembly."

There was much work required in finding leaders for the busy parish, in particular, almost 100 teachers and workers for the three Sunday Schools. Also, finances were a concern. In the first *Bulletin* to be mailed the Rector wrote, "Our Church must have more money, if we are to have a strong program. We are seriously in the red." The Congregation rallied loyally to both needs.

During 1959 the Diocese of Virginia decided to elect a Suffragan Bishop and invited congregations to make nominations. At a meeting of the Vestry November 29 the minutes read, "The clergy were excused from the meeting. Following the assumption of the chair by the Senior Warden, the Vestry adopted the following resolution: 'WHEREAS, it is the opinion of the Vestry of The Falls Church that the Reverend J. Hodge Alves by his ministry at The Falls Church and his experience as a clergyman, as evidenced by the attached biographical sketch, is highly qualified for the office of Suffragan Bishop of the Diocese: now BE IT THEREFORE RESOLVED, that the Vestry of The Falls Church nominates the Reverend J. Hodge Alves for the office of Suffragan Bishop.' "

Six months later, in his first "Report to The Congregation" Mr. Alves said, "Usually a Rector and Congregation have a year or two in which to become acquainted and to adjust to one another before any large program is undertaken. We began our Ministry together in the trying period of a large building program. Therefore, these six months have been full, busy and sometimes bewildering. I believe, however, they have been fruitful and we have accomplished much."

THE LARGE BUILDING PROGRAM IS CONSUMMATED

The Rector was speaking of the most ambitious building program ever undertaken by The Falls Church. A great deal of work had been done since the authorization of a new church by the Annual Meeting, January 11, 1956. Funds had been raised, an architect employed and much study and planning done by the congregation, the Vestry, The New Church Committee and the architect. On November 6, 1957, the Vestry convened in special meeting to hear a critical progress report. Dr. Randal Robertson, Chairman of the New Church Committee, stated that the work had reached a crucial stage; and the architect, Mr. Milton Grigg, was present to explain the situation.

Mr. Grigg told the Vestry that the architects had prepared preliminary plans for a new church. However, as they and the committee had worked together, they had come to realize that a proper church to meet the needs of this large congregation could not be built for the $250,000 indicated. He, therefore, was presenting for serious consideration an "Alternative Plan," which would increase the seating capacity of the old church of 400, continue the colonial building as the center of worship, provide the parish hall facilities required for the Sunday School and other activities, and could be readily accomplished for $250,000. In the church this plan involved the removal of enough of the east wall to allow a chancel of the height of the church to be built on the foundations of the Vestry rooms, the placing of galleries on the south, west and north sides, with stairs ascending on each side from a small narthex at the west door and from an ambulatory in the east, with the choir and organ to be placed in the west gallery. A parish hall of adequate size would then be built further to the east, connecting with the existing buildings. Sacristy and choir areas would be provided between the church and parish house.

After further study the Vestry decided to present this "Alternative Plan" to the Congregation for its consideration. The Senior Warden was instructed to call a meeting of the Congregation and the Committee to prepare an explanatory statement and suitable brochure to aid in the presentation. An excellent brochure was prepared, and a letter sent to every member calling for a meeting and stating, "The Alternative Plan appears to have much merit and your Vestry considers it their duty to bring it and other studies which have been made to the attention of the Congregation."

The Special Meeting of the Congregation heard explanations from the Committee, the Vestry and the architect. There was full opportunity for questions and discussion, but no actions were to be taken. The minutes read, "Some of the comments and questions seemed to favor proceeding with plans for a new church. Others seemed favorable to the alternative approach. Still others seemed noncommittal."

At the next regular Vestry meeting it was decided unanimously "That the Vestry recommends to the Congregation of The Falls Church that the Congregation authorize the Vestry to proceed with the Alternative Plan for expansion as outlined at the Special Meeting of the Congregation on December 13, 1957, which includes alteration of the present church building and construction of a new educational addition."

The Vestry took seriously its responsibility to inform the congregation. At one point an attractive miniature of the church was made by Cdr. C.W. Bunting and a group of the youth, showing exactly how the interior of the church would look. Many members were influenced by the statement that there already had been several restorations involving large interior changes; and that this proposed change, returning the church to its original Georgian style and adding the galleries as planned in 1765, would greatly enhance the beauty of this historic building.

The Annual Meeting of the Congregation, January 13, 1958, was one of the largest ever held. There being no Rector, Harold Spelman, Senior Warden, presided. There was some strong opposition to the Vestry's recommendation, but after a full discussion by all in attendance, the congregation voted 125-53 to authorize the Vestry to proceed with "The Alternative Plan for Expansion."

Sunday, May 31, 1959, was proclaimed "Moving Day." Men, women and youth gathered to move all furnishings and equipment from the church and adjacent rooms to the Parish House so that the contractor might begin work the next day. Even the panelling in the chancel was set up on the stage of the auditorium, which became a church for seven months.

As the interior of the 1767-69 building was stripped, many interesting things were discovered. Mr. Spelman has spoken of some of them in the first half of this book, for proof was found for many previous features and changes mentioned in his chapters. Before the work was begun, it was thought that it might not be necessary to remove all plaster and completely gut the building, but finally this was done so that the brick surfaces could all be waterproofed. Some interesting inscriptions in both pencil and charcoal were uncovered on the plastered surfaces under the wainscoting near the doors and also on some whitewashed surface sections of the wall. These, too, have been mentioned earlier.

The exposed brick masonry was in the English bond. The outside face of these walls above the water table is in Flemish bond. The plaster had been placed directly on the brick. The ceiling plaster was applied on hand split lath, a sample of which is in the Memorials room. The interior cornice was of wood with plaster on hand split lath. Curving wood pieces nailed to the joists provided the half-circle forms to which the lath was nailed. Several joists and beams were patched, but most of the large two-hundred-year old timbers were still sound. Only one or two had to be replaced. Sharing in these discoveries led the Rector to write in the October 18, 1959, *Bulletin*, "All my life I have wished old things could speak. This feeling has come over me many times in recent months, as we have studied, watched and labored with this venerable building known as The Falls Church. What a thrilling story these revered walls could unfold!"

On September 15 at a subsequent meeting of the congregation, with the new Rector presiding, a motion to approve "an additional indebtedness not to exceed $170,000. . .to carry out the building program authorized by the Congregation at its Annual Meeting January 13, 1958," was carried overwhelmingly. There was already a debt for $42,000 on the 1952 parish hall. Arrangements were made with the same lender, Acacia Mutual Life Insurance Co., to consolidate the loan for $212,000 at 5% interest. The Church would now pay $1400 a month for twenty years.

The reorganized Building Committee, with Mr. Robert Hubbell as Chairman, proceeded to arrange for the building of the central section of the Parish House. This beautiful, modern and commodious two-story addition, was to abut the north end of the existing Parish House, and to be connected to the Church by a cloistered porch. The architecture would be in complete harmony with the existing buildings with the roof line low, so as not to dominate the colonial structure. Finally, the addition would contain a small auditorium, six offices, parlor, library, nursery, choir vesting rooms, storage and work rooms and ten large classrooms. The whole would have central heating and air conditioning. Ground was broken on January 4, 1959, and the building was turned over to the Congregation for use October 4, 1959. Through the generosity of the Women of The Falls Church and other donors the whole was attractively and efficiently furnished. This excellent building came to be used eight to twelve hours every day.

The Falls Church was a very busy place during this year. On April 3, 1959, the Wardens, authorized by the Vestry, signed a contract with Earl K. Rosti, Inc., to make the extensive alterations planned for the colonial church; "it being understood that such contract will provide for the work to be done at cost plus a fixed fee of $5000." This included not only the work in the existing buildings, but also a cloistered porch, with adjacent rooms for sacristy, clergy vesting and bath, which would connect all the buildings on the property. Rosti, already at work on the parish house, was to begin this work June 1 and to complete it by Christmas Eve.

The work was substantially completed by Christmas Eve. The Rector wrote of the services held then: "Christmas 1959 will ever be bright in the memory of the Congregation of The Falls Church. That day were held the first festival services in the renewed and enlarged church. The soft glow of the candles and the magnificent new Georgian lighting—the glorious harmony and integrity of our completed restoration, from pews to galleries to sanctuary with its beautiful Queen Anne holy table; all made a fit setting for the glorious services of Christmas."

On January 10, 1960, the Rt. Rev. Frederick D. Goodwin, Bishop of Virginia, knocked on the beautiful west door of the church, until he and the Rector and attending acolytes were admitted by the Wardens, Randal M. Robertson and Thomas B. Pringle. Bishop Goodwin was escorted to the sanctuary where, assisted by the Rev. J. Hodge Alves, Rector, The Rev. Wallace C. Shields, Curate, the Rev. Francis W. Hayes, Jr., Rector 1945-57, and the Rev. W. Leigh Ribble, Rector 1935-54, he proceeded to hold a "Service of Rededication of The Falls Church and Dedication of the Sanctuary, Furnishings and Main Unit of the Parish House." A gracious reception followed this great service.

A sizable group of the congregation and several historical societies had protested "the changing of this historic edifice," but, after seeing the completion, almost everyone was satisfied with the reverent and authentic restoration.

The leaflet of the service listed the two lay groups most responsible for the completion of this large building program:

The Vestry of The Falls Church

Randal M. Robertson, Senior Warden

Jerome W. Shay, Register

John R. Brush

G. Cabell Busick

Charles W. Campbell

Albert K. Dailey

M. Donn Knight, III

Sidney G. Lineker

James T. McBroom

Jack R. McMillen

Thos. B. Pringle, Jr. Warden

Lawrence. W. Harrison, Treasurer

John D.T. Old

Walter H. Morse

G.D.G. Nicolson

Franklyn W. Phillips

V. Devon Mogan

John J. Chew

A. Hubert Fee

The Building Committee

Chairmen: Robert L. Hubbell and Randal M. Robertson

Members and Former Members

Thomas B. Pringle

Jerome W. Shay

Harold J. Spelman

Franklyn W. Phillips

Walter H. Morse

Charles W. Campbell

Jack R. McMillen

John J. Chew

G. Cabell Busick

James T. Rutter

This extensive program of physical development continued for over ten years and cost almost $500,000. The grounds were rounded out by the purchase of the Gorham Tract in 1963 for $15,000. This tract jutted into the front lawn of the Parish House. Brick walks were built, outdoor lighting of colonial lanterns was installed, a well equipped and fenced playyard was built, and the whole was fully landscaped.

When opened, the church was equipped with heating, air conditioning, beautiful hand-made furniture of walnut and oak enamelled white, carpet and magnificent Georgian lighting fixtures. The Altar Guild under the guidance of their chairman, Mrs. L.W. Harrison, took the lead in supplying all other needs. Their standard was that everything must be in keeping with the high quality of what had been done. Service lights, credence tables, flags, a hand-beaten silver altar set of candlesticks, vases and missal stand, a service book, lectern Bible, prayer books, hymnals and additional silver alms basins were among memorial gifts received. Vestments of linen and silks for the Holy Table, Communion Service, lectern and pulpit were designed and sewn. Much of the inspiration came from Wren Chapel of the College of William and Mary.

As a final touch on May 25, 1967, the Schantz Organ Co. of Orrville, Ohio, installed the first pipe organ ever to be in The Falls

Church. The program of dedication said, "The instrument has been specifically designed for The Falls Church with the following needs in mind: (1) to be tonally adequate for The Falls Church building; (2) to function well in the needs of service playing, but flexible enough for recital playing; (3) to enhance but in no way detract from the simple beauty of the building." The seven-hundred pipe instrument is divided into two sections. The Great Organ is exposed on the rail of the West Gallery and the Swell Organ is enclosed in a case on the West Gallery Wall. The quality of the organ is described as "bright, clear and articulate, qualities sought after in an instrument by all organists." The total cost of over $33,000 had already been accumulated in special gifts. The large electronic organ the church had been using was given to Goodwin House, the new Episcopal Home for the Aging. Earlier, the Vestry presented the furniture removed from the church to St. Mark's Mission, Groveton.

AN ERA OF DEVELOPMENT AND MATURING

As soon as Mr. Alves was settled in the Parish, the clergy undertook a total parish visitation. Attendance at services increased and many expressed interest in confirmation. Therefore, classes for all ages were begun in January. The Confirmation Service was held on Whitsunday 1959. The Church *Bulletin* said, "It is a moving experience to see 106 persons solemnly declare their allegiance to Jesus Christ as Lord and Saviour in the vows of the Confirmation Service. The Rector and Curate, who had jointly recruited and trained the candidates, joined in presenting this largest class ever presented in The Falls Church. The Rt. Rev. Robert F. Gibson, Bishop Coadjutor, and the Rt. Rev. Roy Mason, Suffragan, both took part in the 'laying on of hands.' "

During this period the resignation of the Rev. Louis Munroe Bradford was a sad note. Immediately after Easter Mr. Bradford notified the Rector and Vestry that he planned to leave The Falls Church on September 1 after three years as Curate in order to become Rector of a congregation. The Congregation honored Louis and Danie Bradford with a farewell reception and gave their Curate a beautiful private communion service. The Vestry honored Mr. Bradford with a warm minute of appreciation.

The Rev. Wallace C. Shields, Priest-in-Charge of St. Mary's, Bluefield, Virginia, accepted the call of the Rector and Vestry to become Curate of The Falls Church in May. He, his wife, Elsie (Hefner), and their young son arrived September 1, 1959. He immediately went to work in the areas Mr. Bradford had served. It was soon apparent that two clergy were not able to adequately carry the whole work of the parish and that some further help would be needed.

After much study by the clergy and the Christian Education Committee, it was decided that a Director of Christian Education would best meet this need, especially for the large Sunday School. The Vestry authorized the Rector, Superintendent of the Sunday School and Chairman of Christian Education to seek such a person. Miss Alice Whitley, who was first invited to take the position, returned home after trying the large work for a month. In successive years Miss Gertrude Brisbane and Miss Rose Lee Baldwin, both of whom had served in large parishes, became Director of Christian Education, but neither remained much over a year. It was then decided to employ a Sunday School secretary to work under the direction and with the guidance of the superintendent and clergy. Mrs. Roy Franklin was the first to fill this position.

The Rev. Wallace C. Shields accepted the call of St. Mary's, Colonial Beach, Virginia, and resigned as of July 1, 1961. The Congregation said goodbye with a reception and fitting gifts to the young couple.

In May of 1961 the Congregation climaxed an outstanding missionary effort with a memorable evening. Parishioners of every age gathered for a covered dish supper honoring and saying goodbye to three graduating seminary students: Charles Tait, Todd Treft and Philip Turner, who were on their way to Uganda to teach in the Anglican Seminary. The Falls Church gave $1500 toward $50,000 the Seminary was raising to support this venture as The Henry St. George Tucker Memorial.

Through the sixties many leaders of the church from around the world visited and spoke to The Falls Church. Among them were Bishop Zula of the Royal Family of Zulu; Bishop Solomon of Dornakal; Robert Andrews of Fiji; Bishop de Los Reyes, Supreme Bishop of the Philippines Independent Church; Joseph Takabatake of Japan; Henry Okullu of Uganda; Mrs. Virginia Haley of St. Paul's University, Tokyo; Robert Kirby of the church in Australia; Jose Gomez, Dean of the Cathedral in Mexico; and Mrs. Marjorie Leighey, the Congregation's own missionary who taught at St. Agnes School, Kyoto, Japan. Through the years of its history one finds The Falls Church a strong supporter of missions.

Mrs. H. Wells Jones, having served fifteen years as church secretary and desiring "to have time to play with my grandchildren," retired July 1, 1961. The Congregation gave her a reception and presented her a beautiful pair of silver candelabra. (The vital position of church secretary has been filled by a number of competent persons. In 1969 the two secretaries, Mrs. Harold Manning and Mrs. Alan Humphreys, continue to set a high standard.)

One of the highlights of 1961 was the arrival on July 1 of the Rev. James Spilman Petty to become Curate of The Falls Church. Mr. Petty came from St. George's, Stanley, Virginia. He was a graduate of George Washington University and Virginia Theological Seminary and had served in the Army. He, his wife, Nancylee (Bogardus) and their infant son, Stephen, were warmly received and soon became an integral part of the congregation. Mr. Petty quickly proved himself to be a hard worker, excellent preacher and devoted priest. He was especially capable with the young people of the parish.

On Septuagesima Sunday 1962 the resignation of Donald Mori was announced in church. For six years Mr. Mori had been organist and choir director for The Falls Church, in which he had grown up. An accomplished musician and loyal churchman, Don had upheld the fine musical tradition he had inherited from his predecessor and teacher, Percy Burness. The *Bulletin* expressed the high regard and esteem of the congregation for Mr. Mori and wished him an effective ministry for Christ in his field of music.

William H. Snyder came to be organist and choirmaster at the beginning of Lent. He had an M.A. degree and ten years training in music. Under his excellent music leadership and hard work the choirs continued to grow and develop. Mr. Snyder gave invaluable assistance in the planning of the pipe organ, and he has helpfully developed the ministry of music in The Falls Church. The choirs continue to produce outstanding music under his guidance, and the youth choristers win highest awards at the Diocesan Choir Camp regularly.

CANON BAINES AND THE RECTOR EXCHANGE PULPITS

Canon Roger W. Baines, Vicar of St. Peter's, Harrogate, Yorkshire, England, invited the Rector to exchange churches during 1963. It was decided the exchange would cover May, June and July. The Vestry Minutes of September 12, 1962, state, "Concerning an invitation to the Rector from Canon Roger Baines. . .for an exchange May 1 through July. . .and Mr. Alves' plan to visit the Holy Land before his return September 1. . ., The Vestry were of the opinion that such an exchange would be very valuable and they approved it." The Curate agreed to remain one year longer than his contract in order to assist in this plan.

On his return Mr. Alves stated, "As Rector of a venerable Colonial Church, I was delighted to receive the following license to serve:

"We, Frederick Donald, by Divine Providence Lord Archbishop of York, Primate of England and Metropolitan, do by Virtue of the Provision of the Act passed in the Session of Parliament holden in the thirty-seventh year of the Reign of her Majesty Queen Victoria, chapter seventy-seven, intituled 'An act respecting Colonial and certain other clergy,' give and grant this hour Permission that the Reverend Joseph Hodge Alves, who was ordained Deacon on the 29th day of June, 1929, by the Lord Bishop of Alabama and Priest on the 4th day of June, 1930 by the Lord Bishop of Alabama and has produced to us sufficient testimonials from the Lord Bishop of Virginia and has made and subscribed the Declaration required by the said Act to officiate in the Province of York during 1963 on his obtaining the Consent of the Bishop of the Diocese within which such church is situated.

Given under our hand and seal this 17th day of May in the year of Our Lord 1963. And in the second year of our Translation. Donald Ebor."

This certificate is countersigned "Permission to officiate in the Diocese of Ripon. † John Ripon."

In his Annual Report to the congregation in January 1964 the Rector said, "The exchange between Canon Baines and myself proved rich and helpful to both Clergymen and both parishes. The Senior Warden has spoken warmly of the stay of Canon and Mrs. Baines. Mrs. Alves and I had an equally happy experience. We were sincerely received and warmly treated as 'Vicar and Wife' for our three months in Harrogate. The Vicar's Warden and the Curate made a statement, at the time of our leaving, that seems to express the value of this experiment, 'We have learned, through the visit of Mr. and Mrs. Alves, how important it is to live with other people in order to know them. They have walked into our hearts. There is too much water between England and America; and exchanges like this are good for all of us; and so essential in the avoidance of misunderstandings which can arise from time to time.' "

THE FALLS CHURCH DAY SCHOOL ESTABLISHED

A "Church-centered Kindergarten" had been presented as "a challenge for the near future," in the Rector's 1960 Annual Report. On February 14, 1962, the Vestry unanimously approved the recommendations presented by Walter Morse, Chairman of the Christian Educational Committee, "to explore the feasibility of establishing a parochial day school for pre-school age." Mr. Morse and the Rector were asked to set up a committee to study this subject. This ad hoc committee composed of Mr. Morse, chairman, the Rector, Senior

Warden, a vestryman, two parents of Sunday School pupils, two Sunday School teachers, two communicants teaching in public school, a representative from the adult classes and a representative of the Women of the Church, worked for almost one full year. Guidance was sought from the Diocese, the National Church, local churches, schools and school boards. Out of this study came a recommendation for the "Organization and Administration of the Parish Pre-School" and an excellent "Statement of Purpose for a Parochial Day School." Among the statements included in this survey were, "The school must be primarily a Christian school, stressing daily the child's relation with God. . .The teachers must be not only very well qualified professionally, but also acknowledgers of the truth of God,in every branch of learning. . .The school must be open to all children, regardless of religion or race. . .The school should establish a first grade within a year."

On November 28, 1962, the Vestry met in special session to hear a report from its "Committee on the School." Mr. Morse, chairman, presented in writing a careful analysis of the need, purpose, structure and procedure necessary to form such a school. At its February 1963 meeting the Vestry unanimously "authorized activation of a Day School in accordance with the recommendations of the committee. . .and an advance up to $500." The Vestry appointed a Day School Board composed of the Rector as chairman, Mesdames Charles Barrett, Armistead Seldyn and Phillip Stevens, and Messrs. Charles Campbell, Walter Morse and Julien Schrenk. The Rector appointed Walter H. Morse to be Executive Vice-Chairman.

A newspaper notice of July 1962 stated, "The Falls Church (Episcopal), Washington at Fairfax Street in Falls Church, is establishing an Episcopal Day School, a non-profit pre-school for four-and five-year olds. Planned curriculum of religion, social studies, nature, art, reading readiness, manipulative skills and supervised play from 9 to 12 each week day. Accredited teaching staff of Mmes. Josephine Alves, Blanche Fischer, and Caroline Whiting. Registration fee $10. Monthly tuition $25. Opening—September 9, 1963. Phone Mrs. Caroline Whiting, Coordinator." The school opened with 45 pupils. The second year, it added a first grade and in four years it grew to six teachers and 72 pupils. The clergy of the congregation were chaplains to the school and held a weekly service in the church.

REV. PETTY RESIGNS AS CURATE

The *Bulletin* of May 31, 1964, carried on the front page the following announcement: "The Rev. James S. Petty, our Curate, has presented his resignation to the Rector to become effective August

1. Mr. Petty has been called to begin a new work of our church in the Great Falls area." In presenting Mr. Petty's resignation to the Vestry, the Rector spoke in warm appreciation of the support Mr. Petty had given through his three years, of the outstanding leadership he had shown among the youth and of the helpful preparations he had made for the next Curate. In expressing his thanks, Mr. Petty said he would exert his influence to see that the new church at Great Falls would not be named "The Greater Falls Church."

The congregation gave a very well attended reception for the Pettys. The Rector, Vestry and Congregation presented to their Curate a sterling silver private communion service.

Two pieces of good news brought parish receptions in August 1964. On the ninth the Congregation said goodbye to Marjorie Leighey as she left for her work as a missionary teacher in Kyoto, Japan. She was presented a twelve-volume set of the *Interpreters Bible* to help her in her work and a beautiful pen. (A year earlier, another member of the parish, Colonel George Warren, had gone to teach in St. Paul's University, Tokyo.)

The other occasion for a parish reception was the arrival August 15, 1964, of the Rev. William McKinley Duncan, III, to become Curate of The Falls Church. Mr. Duncan was born in Cleveland, Ohio, thirty years before. He attended the University of the South and the University of Texas and received his Bachelor in Divinity from Virginia Theological Seminary. The new Curate had been serving in the Diocese of West Texas as missionary and Dean of the Southern Convocation. He had served two years in the Air Corps. Mr. Duncan, his wife, Jane (Ferrero), and their two children entered quickly into the full life of the parish. He was soon immersed in many activities, especially with the youth and Sunday School.

In his Report to the Congregation some time later Mr. Duncan made an observation that illustrates his keen perception, "The Falls Church Sunday School is no longer bursting at the seams. Registration is just half what it was eight years ago. No longer can we confidently wait for the classrooms to fill up...Young parishes in neighboring areas are beginning to exercise their teaching ministry which, until recently, rested solely with The Falls Church, and we would not push back the clock. With 2300 baptised members we still have a large task in Christian Education before us."

THE FALLS CHURCH IN THE MID-SIXTIES

Stewardship had steadily been one of the concerns of the Rector, Vestry and leaders. A program of education and emphasis on the theology and spiritual basis of Christian Stewardship was bearing fruit as evidenced by words in the Rector's report for 1964. "Our Stewardship Program is growing. At least we approach support of an adequate budget. Mr. Richard Beverley, chairman, announces that 'for 1965 we have 521 adult and 94 youth pledges totalling $102,060, the largest amount ever pledged by this congregation in an anual canvas.' Your Vestry has pledged to give the diocese and world church 21% of the receipts. It is estimated that this will amount to about $20,000. . . ." This advance continued, though with ups and downs. In spite of the tensions of the times, the amount pledged for 1969 was approximately $106,000.

The ferment of the world in the mid-sixties did not escape the church. At the beginning of 1966 the Rector wrote words that spoke to this situation: "1965 has been a year of accomplishment and of tension, within the Church as within the world. War and other social struggles inevitably bring deep concerns and differences. Some within this congregation feel that taking any active part in these struggles, or the debates on them, except to offer prayers for those involved, is a mistake. Others feel the Church must throw its total life into these social struggles of man. Somehow, a congregation must take a vital place in these tremendous movements, but must keep a sane balance that will enable it to be a spiritual home for honest men of varying opinions. The ministry of the Church must always contain the quality of reconciliation. Worship is the heart of a congregation's life, as we have said constantly. It is in this act that we hear God's judgment on each person and the world. It is here that we together seek God's guidance in a changing and confusing day of great promise."

The Falls Church added new dimensions to its total involvement with its Anglican brethren and with all Christians through studying and sharing in "The Mutual Responsibility and Interdependence Movement" of the world Anglican Church. It shared in ecumenical gatherings throughout the community and the area to as broad an extent as possible.

The prayer life of the parish was greatly deepened and increased by a "Lenten Retreat on Prayer," in March 1966, led by the Rev. J. Moulton Thomas, Field Representative of the Anglican Fellowship of Prayer. Mr. Thomas called his presentation "An Insurance Policy for Marriage," which, he said, "is, of course, none other than prayer's undergirding of the 101 'human' aspects of marriage." Six couples had a life-enlarging experience and returned to form a vital Couples Prayer Group. From this grew Prayer Groups for men and for women, and in 1968 a month-long series of Prayer Power Workshops that involved twelve congregations and resulted in a Clergy Prayer Group.

In his notes on February 27, 1966, the Rector said, "It is with regret that I announce the resignation of our Curate. The Rev. William M. Duncan has accepted a call to become the Rector of St. John's Church, Camden, Arkansas, as of May 1st. He will be leaving Falls Church on April 15. Mr. Duncan, as our Curate for almost two years, has been a strong helper to the Rector in all the work of the parish, especially that with youth and education. He and his lovely family have been a vital part of the life and work of the congregation of The Falls Church."

The Vestry and congregation gave a reception on Palm Sunday "honoring the Rev. and Mrs. William M. Duncan as they leave to take up a new ministry." They also presented to the young priest a beautiful private communion set.

The Rector and Wardens set to work again to find an Assistant. At the Rector's request the Vestry authorized "an increase in salary not to exceed $700." The minutes of April 13 state "The Rector announced that the Rev. R. Robert Ismay, presently Rector of St. Andrew's Church, Princess Ann, Md., has accepted the call to be Assistant Minister effective June 1, 1966. This has been approved by Bishop Gibson. Mr. Ismay is a graduate of Syracuse University, Colgate-Rochester Divinity School and Virginia Seminary. He began his ministry in the Methodist Church and entered the Episcopal ministry about ten years ago." The Ismays and their three sons were warmly welcomed at a formal reception Sunday, June 19, given by the Rector, Vestry, Women of The Church, and the congregation.

The Virginia Seminary approached the Rector and Vestry with the request to assist in their "Second Century Fund" begun early in 1966. It was suggested that instead of a full campaign The Falls Church might undertake to double their usual annual giving through 1967-69. This would mean $1000 per year. The Rector, Vestry and congregation were glad to undertake this for its dear friend of many years. During these three years almost $4000 was given to the Seminary.

The Rev. R. Robert Ismay resigned as Assistant Rector, effective June 15, 1967. The Rector, Vestry and congregation gave a reception for the Rev. and Mrs. Ismay on the Sunday before their leaving. The Rector said in the *Bulletin*, "The prayers of Priest and People go with the Ismays as they go forth to their new work in McIlhany Parish, Albermarle County."

The Rector and Vestry decided to study thoroughly the whole matter of Assistant Priests. An ad hoc committee of Senior Warden, Register, Chairman of Christian Education and Chairman of Missions was appointed "to study, in cooperation with the Rector, the needs of the parish and abilities that should be sought in an assistant." This Committee, after six months study produced an excellent brochure, "Staff Needs of The Falls Church." The findings and recommendations of this 25-page document included a thoughtful section, "The Core Ministry." It particularly called for an upgrading of the whole concept of the assistant and recommended that the parish should seek a mature experienced priest to share the core ministry. Because of the wait of six months for the completion of this study and the difficulty in finding this kind of priest, the parish was a full year without an assistant. Two priests were employed part time and gave invaluable aid to the Rector in this difficult situation: The Rev. Ronald Merrix, who was one of the first residents at Goodwin House, and the Rev. Gerald H. Nolting, a priest working in business.

The Rector in consultation with the Ad Hoc Committee, approached a score of men. He wrote each that he and the parish were seeking "not a Curate but an Associate who would have responsibilities comparable to the Rector and commensurate with his job and would receive adequate remuneration. He would share in the total ministry, preaching approximately half the time and counselling where indicated."

The good results of this year of work were chronicled in the Rector's Annual Report, January 1969. "The coming of the Rev. Robert T. Copenhaver to be our Associate Priest is one of the most heartening developments of 1968. We studied and explored the field for several months before we found him and received his consent to join our staff. Bob and his lovely wife, Mimi, and their three fine boys have quickly become an important part of our parish family. He is sharing the total ministry of this large parish and is being particularly effective with our young people and young families."

"From The Rector's Desk," a special news section of The *Bulletin,* for June 16, 1968, said in part: "This Sunday marks the tenth anniversary of our life together as Rector and People. These have been full, busy and sometimes difficult years. They have also been fruitful years in the long ministry of The Falls Church. Together we have influenced many people for Jesus Christ. Thousands have entered in some way into the life of this congregation. . .588 have been baptised and 936 confirmed during these ten years. We now list 1374 baptised persons and 1215 communicants. The Sunday School has 427 pupils and 65 officers and teachers. Much has been done to meet the need for physical facilities and educational opportunities."

The vital ministry of the laity of The Falls Church was a large element in making this work possible. The Vestry has shown devotion and consecrated effort through the many years of the parish's life. The Women of The Falls Church also gave devoted service in many ways. The growing maturity of the congregation was evidenced in the election of women to the Vestry and the Diocesan Council. Mrs. Ruth Reeves was elected in 1968 to be the first woman ever to serve as vestryman. At the 1969 Annual Meeting Mrs. L.W. Harrison was the second to be elected. The Vestry then elected as one of its three delegates to the 1969 Council of the Diocese Mrs. Allen Long, the president of the Women of The Church.

Through special working guilds of both women and men many good works have been done: The Library Guild, composed of a score of well trained and dedicated women, has built up an effective and much used library of 1500 volumes. The Layreaders Guild, The Altar Guild, the Ushers Guild and the Guild of The Christ Child all have extended this lay ministry.

The Rector had written, "So many groups and persons, both known and unknown have shared in our development it would take volumes to tell about them all." Their number is legion, but we would especially mention from these ten years Richard Beverly, Florence Harrison, Albert Lester, Gordon Nicolson and Julian Slade as representatives of a large group of loyal sons and daughters.

The parish, under the leadership of Walter Tinsley, entered enthusiastically into the Diocesan and Parish Survey for a year of intensive self study, beginning December 1, 1967. The study was guided by The General Division of Research and Field Study of the National Church. Two hundred and twenty-seven members of the congregation participated in this study. Concerning this effort, the National Division in its findings said, "The local group is to be commended for the quality and extent of the material which it compiled for the study. This group exhibited great knowledge of and concern for this church, its problems, its challenges and its opportunities for the future. It is the hope of the General Division of Research and Field Study, that the interest, enthusiasm and dedication which characterized this study will likewise be focused on the task of understanding and implementing the recommendations of this survey."

As a result of this thorough study, the Bishop appointed a Steering Committee and asked each parish to appoint a Parish Planning Committee of eight "concerned persons not in a policy-making position." Again, Walter Tinsley took the lead with Bruce Scott as co-chairman and David Williams as secretary. The other members were Richard Welles, Robert Hubbell, Mrs. Franklin Thackrey, Mrs. Richard Walton and William Cooksey. Radcliffe Park later replaced Mr. Hubbell. The basic task of this committee was "to apply the formal process of planning to appropriate issues, subjects or matters of concern involving the future of The Falls Church and its mission."

In the Annual Report given January 1965 the Rector called attention to the fact that "1969 will mark the Two Hundredth Anniversary of the completion of our church building. We should recognize this properly. We must appoint a special committee to make plans." At a regular meeting of the Vestry December 1966 on request of the Rector "It was moved that the Vestry designate 1969 as the Bicentennial of the building of The Falls Church and authorize an appropriate celebration." The Rector asked the Senior Warden, Register, Treasurer, and two lay persons to meet with him as an Ad Hoc Committee to choose a Bicentennial Committee and set up plans for a celebration.

The results of the Ad Hoc Committee's work was given in a report to the Vestry in April 1968, in which it nominated the Bicentennial Committee listed in the front of this book. The Vestry unanimously appointed this Committee and charged it "to prepare for a proper celebration of the 200th Anniversary of the completion of our beautiful and historic church, culminating in festival services on Sunday, May 18, 1969, with the Bishop of the Protestant Episcopal Church in the U.S.A. as the Preacher."

The Planning Committee presented its first full report to the Congregation at the Annual Meeting, January 15, 1969. The Congregation then joined the Vestry in approving the Committee's "Statement of Purpose," the words of which point to the future and seem fitting to close this brief history.

"The Falls Church will strive to enkindle, map and develop new missionary and evangelistic programs. These programs will be strengthened by emphasizing the Christian community total stewardship, personal witness and the many needs of the community, nation and world.

The Congregation will make a continual effort to evaluate and promote orderly and adequate movement toward accomplishing these goals."

96

bibliogRaphy

Andrews, Matthew Page, Compiler. *The Women of the South in War Times.* Norman, Remington, 1920.

Goodwin, W.A.R. *The History of the Theological Seminary in Virginia.* New York: Edwin S. Gorham, 1923.

Meade, William, Bishop. *Old Churches, Ministers and Families of Virginia.* (Originally published 1857.) Baltimore: Genealogical Publishing Co., 1966.

Rawlings, James Scott. *Virginia's Colonial Churches.* Richmond, Va.: Garret and Massie, 1963.

Slaughter, Philip. *The History of Truro Parish in Virginia.* Edited by the Rev. Edward L. Goodwin. Philadelphia: Geo. W. Jacobs and Co., 1908.

Steadman, Melvin Lee, Jr. *Falls Church By Fence and Fireside.* Falls Church, Va.: Falls Church Public Library, 1964.

Stewart, Charles A. "The Falls Church 1733-1940." Unpublished manuscript, two volumes typewritten, 1940.

————. *A Virginia Village.* J.H. Newell, 1904.

appenòices

APPENDIX A

The First Levy Laid for Truro Parish

At a Vestry held for Truro Parish on the 12 day of October 1733 Present, John Heryford, Edward Ems, Church Wardens, Wm. Godfrey, John Sturman, Michl. Ashford, Edward Barry and Richard Osborn. Then the Vestry proceeded to lay the levy.

Truro Parish	Dr.	Tobo.
To the Rev. Mr. Lawrence DeButts		8660
To Edw. Barry, and acct.		3350
To Catisby Cocke		344
" Richard Blackburn, in part for building the Church		16,750
" Charles Christmas for being Sexton		600
" Hugh West, for burying Thos. Gahagan		100
" Mary Cofer, for burying James Howson		300
" Thomas Sympson, for maintaining Oliver Row		400
" Elizabeth Ward, for burying Sarah Holmes		400
" Wm. Brookshire, " " Wm. Neale		400
" Wm. Hall, Junr., for nursing a poor child		515
" Thomas West, for burying Henry Hudson		400
" David Jones, for tarring the church		400
" Thos. Lewis, for burying Joseph Barnes		400
" Tobacco towards purchase of a gleeb		5,000
" John Sturman, for drawing bonds		400
To Wm. Godfrey, for delinquents		1,000
To do for making shutters for the windows		1,000
To Capt. Fras. Aubrey, towards building the Chappell above Goose Creek		2,500
To Sallary for collecting and casks		3,372
Supra. Crd.	lbs.	45,399
By 681 tythables at 67 lb. tobacco nett per pole		45,399

"Ordered, that Edward Ems and Edward Barry receive from each tythable person within this parish 67 lbs. of tobacco, it being the nett of the parish levy for the present year.

Jeremiah Bronaugh, Wm. Peake, John Farguson, and Thos. Lewis being this day chosen members of this Vestry, in the room of several deceased members, and they having taken the oaths appointed by law, and subscribed the test, took their places therein accordingly. Present—Jeremiah Bronaugh, William Peake, John Farguson and Thomas Lewis.

Ordered that Joseph Johnson be reader at the new church and the Chappell above Goose Creek, and that 1300 pounds of tobacco be levied for him at the laying of the next parish levy, provided he does his duty in his office."

John Heryford, Church Warden
Edward Ems, Church Warden

APPENDIX B

LEVIES AND CHURCH WARDENS

Year Laid	Tith-ables	Tobacco Per Poll	Total	Church Wardens Appointed For Ensuing Year	Included For Bldgs. and Lands
1733	681	80	54,480	John Heryford, Edward Ems	24,250
1734	676	72	48,728	Jeremiah Bronaugh, Edward Ems	19,000
1735	732	7	10,707	" " " "	4,000
1736	858	61	50,768	Jeremiah Bronaugh, Thos. Lewis	20,000
1737	880	42½	38,383	Thos. Lewis, Edward Barry	16,900
1738	1013	45	45,872	Thos. Lewis, Edward Barry	—
1739	1002	38	38,076	Thos. Lewis, Edward Barry	4,000
1740	1106	33	34,498	John Colvil, Edward Barry	
1741	1124	36	40,464	Jeremiah Bronaugh, Edward Barry	
1742	1331	23	30,613	" "	
1743	1372	25	34,300	Jeremiah Bronaugh, John Sturman	
1744	1476	25	37,388	John West, Lewis Elzey	4,000
1745	1550	25	42,341	John Minor, " "	12,250
1746	1669	27	46,068	John Minor, Hugh West	12,250
1747	1745	19	35,546	Andrew Hutchinson, Richard Osborn	
1748	1687	27	45,009	Edward Ems, Richard Boggess	
1749	1240[1]	21	27,357	Hugh West, (Jeremiah Bronaugh, decd. (George Mason	
1750	1221	32	42,157	Charles Broadwater, James Hamilton	12,000
1751	1225	34	41,650	William Payne, Sr. Daniel McCarty	10,000
1752	1272	50	63,600	Chas. Broadwater, Abraham Barnes	34,049
1753	1423	45	64,170	Daniel McCarty, Thos. Wren	34,225
1754	1470	34	50,480	Robert Boggess, John Turley	13,500
1755	1412	25	36,631	John West, George Mason	
1756	1400	30	42,373	John West, Chas. Broadwater	
1757	1382	25	35,698	John West, Wm. Payne, Sr.	
1758	1419	23	32,637	John West, Daniel McCarty	
1759	1537	22	33,814	Thomas Wren, Robert Bogess	
1760	1613	20	32,260	" " " "	
1761	1589	26	41,314	William Payne, Jr., Henry Gunnell	
1762	1616	22	35,552	" " " " "	

---

[1]Cameron Parish cut off in 1748.

1763	1807	37	64,860	Geo. Wm. Fairfax, George Washington 30,000
1764	1879	32	60,128	Daniel McCarty, William Payne, Jr. ....

Falls Church to Fairfax Parish

1765	1013	47	47,611	Wm. Payne, Jr., John West 32,720
1766	1017	65	66,105	Wm. Adams, John Dalton 31,189
1767	1121	57	63,897	Edw. Duling, Chas. Broadwater 26,000
1768	1149	60	68,940	Daniel French, Thos. Shaw...................28,784
1769	1205	50	60,250	Townsend Dade, James Wren...................19,996
1770	1248	59	73,630	John West, Wm. Gunnell 21,690
1771	1282	50	64,100	Wm. Payne, Jr., Wm. Adams 19,020
1772	1361	45	61,295	John Dalton, Edw. Duling.....................21,660
1773	1385	54	74,790	Chas. Broadwater, Wm. Gunnell 20,477
1774	1424	40	60,900	Townsend Dade, Wm. Gunnell................18,959
1775	1500	20	30,120	Richard Sandford, James Wren.................
1776	1250[2]	39	48,750	Wm. Payne, Jr., John Dalton 16,000
1777	1278	25	30,672	Wm. Payne, Jr., Richard Conway.............
1778	1221	10	12,210	Wm. Payne, Jr., Chas. Alexander.............
1779	1286	13	16,830	Wm. Payne, Jr., Richard Conway.............
1780	1415	20	28,300	Wm. Payne, Jr., Wm. Herbert ....
1781	1377	26	35,802	Wm. Payne, Jr., Wm. Herbert ....
1782	1400	22	30,800	Chas. Alexander, John Hunter ....
1783	1600	12	19,200	James Wren, Wm. Brown ....
1784	1627[3]	14	22,778	Robert T. Hooe, Wm. Payne III ....

CHURCH WARDENS OF FAIRFAX PARISH
AFTER THE DISESTABLISHMENT

1785	Robert T. Hooe, Wm. Payne, III
1786-90	Wm. Brown, Wm. Payne, III
1791-95	Wm. Payne, III, Roger West
1796	Wm. Payne, III, J.B. Nichols
1797	Philip Fendall, Wm. Herbert

CHURCH WARDENS OF THE FALLS CHURCH.
AS A SEPARATE CONGREGATION IN FAIRFAX PARISH

1873	George Porter, Sackett Duryea
1874	George Porter, Ely Burgess
1875	George Porter, W.H. Plunkett
1876-77	George Porter, Cassius F. Lee
1878-82	Cassius F. Lee, S.D. Tripp
1883-90	Cassius F. Lee, James M. Mason
1890-93	James M. Mason, J.B. Hodgkin
1893-95	J.M. Mason, G.D. Nicolson
1895-96	James M. Mason, Wm. E. Parker
1896-97	J.M. Mason, Geo. D. Nicolson
1897-99	James M. Mason, S.D. Tripp
1899-	
1902	S.D. Tripp, Wm. F. Edmonds
1902-03	S.D. Tripp, Charles A. Marshall
1903-05	S.D. Tripp, Wm. E. Parker
1905-06	S.D. Tripp, J.T. Unverzagt
1906-08	S.D. Tripp, Wm. E. Parker
1908-09	S.D. Tripp, J.M. Smoot
1909-15	S.D. Tripp, Chas. A. Stewart
1916-17	Chas. A. Stewart, G. Nicolson
1917	C.A. Stewart, C.A. Marshall
1918-20	Chas. A. Stewart, G. Nicolson
1920-21	S.H. Styles, Gordon Nicolson
1921-22	Julian Slade, Gordon Nicolson
1922-23	Gordon Nicolson, Julian Slade
1923-24	J.H.C. Valentine, Julian Slade
1924-27	J.T. Unverzagt, Gen. R. Lane
1927-32	J.T. Unverzagt, C.A. Stewart
1932-35	C.A. Stewart, Fred J. Huber
1935-37	C.A. Stewart, Earl B. Stiff
1938-46	C.A. Stewart, H.J. Spelman
1947	R.C. Horne, T.B. Pringle

[2]Approved March 1777. . .The last levy for support of Church.
[3]Approved March 1785. . .The last levy.

1948-49	H.J. Spelman, A.H. Lester	1960	R.L. Hubbell, John J. Chew
1950	H.J. Spelman, T.B. Pringle	1960-61	H.J. Spelman, John J. Chew
1951	T.B. Pringle, A.H. Lester	1962	H.J. Spelman, R.C. Beverley
1952	H.J. Spelman, W.M. Herring	1963	John J. Chew, R.C. Browning
1953-54	H.J. Spelman, T.B. Pringle	1964	H.J. Spelman, R.C. Browning
1955	R.M. Robertson, T.B. Pringle	1965	H.J. Spelman, John J. Chew
1956	R.M. Robertson, H.J. Spelman	1966	H.J. Spelman, R.C. Beverley
1957-58	H.J. Spelman, T.B. Pringle	1967-68	R.M. Robertson, John J. Chew
1959	R.M. Robertson, T.B. Pringle	1969	R.L. Hubbell, John J. Chew

Fairfax Parish was discontinued in 1968, and The Falls Church became a separate congregation in a new Falls Church Parish.

THE BICENTENNIAL COMMITTEE

Lee M. Rhoads, Chairman
Mrs. Harvey Vogel, Secretary
The Rev. J.H. Alves
Robert C. Browning
The Rev. Robert T. Copenhaver
Mrs. L.W. Harrison

Robert L. Hubbell
Mrs. Ruth C. Reeves
Randal M. Robertson
William H. Snyder
Harold J. Spelman
Dabney T. Waring

THE VESTRY FOR 1969

Robert L. Hubbell, Senior Warden
John J. Chew, Junior Warden
Allen A. Long, Register
David P. Beatty, Treasurer
Robert C. Browning
Howard H. Dewhirst
Lawrence W. Harrison,
   Honorary Treasurer
Mrs. Lawrence W. Harrison
Harrison D. Hutson

Harold Manning
Clarence J. MacNichols
Glenn E. Peil
Mrs. Ruth C. Reeves
Julien R. Schrenk
Bruce M. Scott
Harold J. Spelman,
   Senior Warden Emeritus
Harvey O. Vogel
Dabney T. Waring

APPENDIX C

READERS AND CLERKS AT FALLS CHURCH

TRURO PARISH

Joseph Johnson	1734-1742
Walter English	1743
John Barry	1744-1745
	(Incl. Pohick)
John Wybird Dainty	1745-1753
William Donaldson	1754-1755
John Lumley	1756-1758
Thomas Lewis	1759-1760
John Barry	1761-1765
	(For 3 churches)

FAIRFAX PARISH

Thomas Wren	1765-1767 dec.
Benjamin West	1767-1772
John Ball	1773-1776
Wm. Carlin	Aug. 1787-Aug. 1789

(Called Readers until 1738, after that Clerks)

SEXTONS AT THE FALLS CHURCH

TRURO PARISH

Thomas Bennet	1736-1743 decd.
Mary Bennet	1743-1755 decd.
John Palmer	1755-1758
Gerard Trammel	1759-1765

FAIRFAX PARISH

Gerard Trammel	1765-1776
Gerard Trammel	Aug. 1787-Aug. 1789

SERVING VESTRY HOUSE

Gerard Trammel   1767-1785

APPENDIX D

MARCH 17, 1766 SPECIFICATIONS FOR THE VESTRY HOUSE AT THE FALLS CHURCH

The dimensions of the Vestry House are as follows, viz; that it shall be 16 feet square with an outside chimney. Planked above and Below to be covered three feet with red oak shingles. The joints to be beaded, the upper floor planed below the door rabbitted and beaded, a sash window with eight lights. The floor to be laid with pine plank. The roof, sides and gable ends to be tarred, the pitch to be 9 feet, a back and hearth to be made of clay. The whole to be framed and finished in a workmanlike manner by the first of November next for two thousand five hundred pounds of transfer tobacco. Henry Darne, Undertaker.

APPENDIX E

SPECIFICATIONS FOR THE CHURCHES
(From Fairfax Vestry Minutes of January 1, 1767)

The churches at the Falls and Alexandria to be 28 feet from the foundation, that is 3 bricks and a half to the sleepers, 3 bricks to the water table and two and one half from thence. The Quoins and arches to be rubbed brick; the pediments to the doors rubbed work in the Tuscan order. The outside of the wall to be done with place bricks. The mortar to be two thirds lime and one sand, the inside half lime and half sand, the isles to be laid with tyle or flags; the lower windows to contain eighteen lights each of 9 x 11, and the upper windows 12 each, besides the compass head, the sashes of the lower windows to hang with weights and pulleys and to be clear of sap; to have medallion cornish under the eaves, the roof to have three pair of principal rafters, or as the workmen call it a principal roof to be framed in the best manner and to be covered with one inch pine or poplar plank laid close to shingle on, the shingles to be made of the best juniper cypress, three quarters of an inch thick, eighteen inches long, and to show six inches. The floors to be laid with inch and a quarter pine plank and to be raised four inches above the isles. The pews to be 3 feet and 6 inches high besides the coping with doors to all. To be neatly wainscoted, with quarter round both sides, and raised panel on one, and to be neatly capped with some handsome moulding—the seats to be 12 x 13 inches broad, the outdoors to be folding and in width. . . .feet, hung with proper hinges, locks and barrs, to be raised panelled on both sides, locust sills to the frame and architrave—the altar piece, pulpit and canopy to be completed in Ionic order. The walls and ceiling to be well plastered with three coats, and with a cove cornish—the whole to be neatly painted and finished in the best manner—the isles to be six feet.

APPENDIX F — THE LAST LEVY

At a Vestry held for the Parish of Fairfax at the Vestry House the 17th day of March, 1785.

Present: Revd. David Griffith William Herbert
Chas. Broadwater George Gilpin   Gm. Vestrymen
James Wren William Brown
Henry Darne Robert T. Hooe ⎱ C. Wardens
John Hunter William Payne ⎰

Fairfax Parish	Dr.
To amt brought forward	13,666
To Thomas Dayley, for keeping Zalph Bryan ....4 mos.	400

To Nelson Reed, for keeping John Young	4 mos.	400
To Sarah Mason		100
To Gerrard Trammel, for attending Vestry	4 mos.	100
To amount carried over		14,666
To Geo. Minor, Clerk of Vestry		200
To John Adams to keeping Susannah Lester	4 mos.	200
To Joseph Burgess for his support		100
To Susannah Linsay, for the poore	4 mos.	586
To Francis Summers, for keeping a poor woman	4 mos.	153
To Eliza Edwards		100
To Elizabeth Payne		250
To Henry Biggs and wife		250
To Wm. Shakespeare, for keeping a poore child		282
To Margaret Hardy		266
To Ananiar Payne for keeping John Henly & wife	4 mos.	533
To William Fraser for keeping the poore	4 mos.	840
Mary Hagan for support of Rebecca Gidding	9 mos.	600
To Wm. Hunt for keeping a poore woman and child	4 mos.	393
To Susannah Thrift, for keeping Mary Watson	4 mos.	286
To Wm. Lyles & Co. for keeping a poor woman		125
William Herbert for a coffin		136
William Miller, for keeping Stephen Snell	6½ wks.	234
Doctor Wm. Brown, for visiting the poore		345
Hugh Middleton, for keeping and burying a poor woman		208
		21,060
To Fraction in Collectors hands		352
To 6 pr. ct. Com. 22778 lb. Tobacco		1,366
By 1627 tythables at 14 lbs. tobacco per pole		22,778

Wm. Brown produced his account of 2 p. 8 s. Ordered that the Church Wardens pay the said sum to the said Brown. Col. Robert T. Hooe and William Payne, Church Wardens, produce an account from Wm. Hartshorne by which appears they had sold him the balance of tobacco which remained in the Sheriff's hands last November, and which they were ordered to sell, and also appears from the acct. that there remains in the hands of Mr. Hartshorne the sum of 13 p. 18 s. 11½ d. which it is now ordered shall be appropriated to supply the "exigencies of the Poore at the discretion of the Church Wardens." Then follow the listing of some 18 indentures, including "an indenture between the Church Wardens of Fairfax Parish and John Chew binding John Reynolds, fifteen years old July 20, 1783."

APPENDIX G

MINISTERS WHO SERVED THE FALLS CHURCH

IN TRURO PARISH	IN FAIRFAX PARISH
May 1733—Sept. 1734	Dec. 1765—June 1778
The Rev. Lawrence DeButts	The Rev. Townsend Dade
Oct. 1735—Sept. 1736	Dec. 1778—Feb. 1779
The Rev. James Keith	The Rev. Wm. West
Oct. 1736—Jan. 1737	Feb. 1779—Aug. 1789
John Holmes	The Rev. David Griffith
Feb. 1737—Aug. 1737	March 1790—July 1792
Joseph Blumfield	The Rev. Bryan Fairfax
Aug. 1737—Jan. 1765	Oct. 1792—circa 1800
Charles Green	The Rev. Thos. Davis

As a separate congregation in Fairfax Parish:

1832-36	Professors and students of the Seminary
1836-42	The Rev. Edw. R. Lippitt
Oct. 1842-44	The Rev. R.T. Brown
1845-52	The Rev. Wm. F. Lockwood
Oct. 1852-55	Professors May and Packard and students
Jan. 1855-June 1861	The Rev. R.T. Brown
1866-73	Professors and students of the Seminary
May 1874-June 1876	The Rt. Rev. Horatio Southgate
Sept. 1877-May 1878	The Rev. John McGill
Nov. 1878-Dec. 1889	The Rev. Frank Page
Aug. 1890-June 1892	The Rev. J. Cleveland Hall
Dec. 1892-Aug. 1895	The Rev. R.A. Castleman
Sept. 1895-Oct. 1899	The Rev. John McGill
Nov. 1899-Mar. 1908	The Rev. Geo. S. Somerville
Sept. 1908-Nov. 1912	The Rev. W.S. Callender
Mar. 1913-Sept. 1913	The Rev. John McGill
Sept. 1913-Mar. 1917	The Rev. A.G. Grinnan
June 1917-July 1931	The Rev. R.A. Castleman
July 1932-Oct. 1934	The Rev. C.S. McClellan
Mar. 1935-Apr. 1945	The Rev. W.L. Ribble
July 1945-Apr. 1957	The Rev. F.W. Hayes
June 1958—	The Rev. J.H. Alves

Fairfax Parish was discontinued in 1968, and The Falls Church became a separate congregation in the new Falls Church Parish.

Prior to 1917 all ministers served other nearby churches also.

inðex